GROWING
MINIATURE
AND
PATIO ROSES

'Cream Puff'

Dawn & Barry Eagle

CASSELL

'Lemon Twist'

Cassell Publishers Limited
Wellington House, 125 Strand
London WC2R 0BB

First published in Great Briatin 1996
in association with
David Bateman Limited
Tarndale Grove, Albany Business Park, Bush Road
Albany, North Shore City, Auckland, New Zealand

Distributed in the United States by Sterling Publishing Co. Inc,
387 Park Avenue South, New York, NY 10016, USA

British Library Cataloguing in Publication Data
A Catalogue record for this book is available from the British
Library

ISBN 0-304-34836-8

Printed in Hong Kong by Colorcraft Ltd

Contents

INTRODUCTION

'San Jose Sunshine'

IT was easy to grow roses when roses were just roses; but then there were hybrid teas and floribundas, miniature and patio roses, shrub and ground cover roses, old roses and English roses. Even with their differences these are still all roses; it can become rather confusing.

Miniature roses are easy. They are small, with small flowers and small leaves, but not necessarily small in stature. The shortest miniature roses may only be 10 or 15 cm high while others reach to a metre and more, with climbing miniatures two and more metres tall. Whatever their height, the flowers and leaves remain small, the stems thin and the distance between the leaves short. Miniature means small flowers, not small plants.

Patio roses are more difficult. It is a commercial term which means different things

to different people. One thing that most are agreed upon is that the flowers, leaves and growth form are larger than those of true miniatures but not really large enough to be floribundas. It is sometimes difficult to draw a dividing line between miniature and patio roses, and we have seen a mixed bed of floribundas and patio roses where there was very little difference between plant and flower size regardless of type. Think of patio roses as larger miniatures and you won't be far wrong. For this reason, in this book, when talking of the care, cultivation and propagation of miniature roses we are including patio roses as well.

Some other roses meet the requirements of small flowers and small leaves. There are miniature climbers, so why not patio clim-

'Loving Touch'

4

bers with slightly larger flowers and leaves? Many of the newer ground cover roses have flowers and leaves which would allow them to be included with miniature and patio roses. Shrub roses tend to have more flowers on shorter stems than the usual bush roses, some are really miniature or patio shrubs with small flowers and leaves. Miniature and patio roses cover a range of types besides the bush form that we usually think of.

Nevertheless, roses are still roses and are all easy to grow. While they may come in a

'Why Not'

variety of types with varying characteristics and descriptions, they still demand the same basic requirements and attention, and we need to be aware of these variations and choose those roses that best suit our purposes and the space available. Miniature and patio roses fit admirably into any garden and especially today's modern smaller gardens. Grow and enjoy them in all their variety and forms.

Chapter 1

IN THE BEGINNING

'Sea Foam'

THERE seems to be a misunderstanding about the relationship between miniature and patio roses and other roses, almost as though a miniature rose were some bonsai or dwarfed form of a larger rose. As a consequence questions like, 'Do you have 'Loving Memory' as a miniature rose?' are often asked. Perhaps the hope is for some secret process which reduces size, as 'Loving Memory' is a large red hybrid tea, but no treatment or cultural practice such as spraying or pruning can convert it or any other rose into a miniature. In the same way, gross feeding will not make a patio rose into a floribunda. You cannot change one type of rose into another.

Where did those first miniature roses come from? It is usually best to start at the beginning.

Roses have existed for thousands of years. Early engravings show roses, and the ancient writings of the Greeks, Romans and Chinese tell of roses and their use, and trade in roses and rose products. The earliest roses are the species roses, found originally across Europe and Asia into China and Japan and also in North America. The names of species roses begin *Rosa* (often abbreviated to *R.*) and so, to name a few, we have *R. eglanteria, R. canina* and *R. gallica,* of England, France and western Europe and *R. carolina* of North America. Many are single with just the five basic petals of the rose and most are pink. Others are so old that their origins are unknown and they are often thought of as species. These include the Albas and Damask roses which were known in Europe in the seventeenth and eighteenth centuries. They originated in Europe and Asia Minor and were

R. chinensis minima

spread widely by merchants trading around the Mediterranean more than 2000 years ago. They were carried by soldiers and officials to the far-flung reaches of the Roman Empire, and knights returning from the crusades brought them home with them. Known for their medicinal value, they were grown and nurtured in monastery herbal gardens and eventually carried by the Church to the Americas. And they were planted in the manor gardens of the new merchant class. Most of these roses had something in common. They only flowered once in the spring and early summer.

Among them were some small roses. Still grown today is *R. parvifolia* or 'Pompon de Bourgogne' the Burgundy Rose, with its tiny dark pink to purple rosette-shaped blooms on bushes less than a metre high. Of later date was *R. centifolia pomponia*, better known as 'Rose de Meaux'. There are two forms, one with pink and the other with white 2-cm blooms.

European settlement in North America and sea trade with Asia around the southern tip of Africa saw a wide variety of new plants being brought into England and France. Towards the end of the eighteenth century the first few of a new family of roses arrived. Later to be grouped as *R. chinensis,* the rose from China, their original home, they were to be of great importance to modern roses as they flowered continuously through the spring and summer.

One of these roses had small pink flowers on willowy stems with small leaves. It was smaller than the others and eventually became known as the small rose from China, *R. chinensis minima*. This and seedlings from it were the first of the true miniature roses. No-one really knows the true background to these roses. Some early reports suggest that they came from Mauritius, but if so, Mauritius was almost certainly just a staging post in the long sea journey from China around the southern tip of Africa. They may have been from a small variety which occurred naturally in the wild but if this is the case, it has never again been discovered. They may have occurred in cultivation; remember that the Chinese had been growing roses for many years.

At first they were called Fairy Roses and they must have been popular for some years as rose nurseries of that era list several of them, all in shades of pink, and Redouté, that great French painter of the time, includes two of them in his folio. They were treated as novelties, grown in pots in the new conservatories, and possibly considered too delicate to be grown as a garden plant in the open.

Then they seemed to disappear for a time. It was not until 1917, when a French climber found a small rose growing in a pot on a window ledge of a cottage in the Swiss Alps, that they appeared once again in rose literature. It was thought to be a new rose species and was named *Rosa rouletti* after the discoverer. It was described at the time as very small, 'a minuscule shrub, five centimetres high, bushy and covered with small Roses not exceeding one and a half centimetres broad', and deep pink in colour. It may have been the rose 'Pompon de Paris', a variety of *R. chinensis minima* sold in the Paris street markets of the 1830s and 1840s as a flowering pot plant. It was almost certainly a remnant from the Fairy Roses of the early 1800s. This rediscovery created a new interest in small roses.

Another similar rose was found growing in an old garden in England and named 'Oakington Ruby'. Rose breeders in Europe and North America began examining their

R. rouletti

potential as a new class of rose. It took time, but eventually new seedlings appeared. Among the first of these new miniature roses was 'Peon', raised by Jan de Vink of Holland, and renamed 'Tom Thumb' when it crossed the Atlantic to America, where it was released in 1936. These three roses, *rouletti*, 'Tom Thumb' and 'Oakington Ruby', form the basis of all modern miniature roses.

Much of the development of miniature roses was done in the United States by Ralph Moore. Working at his nursery in California in the 1930s, he began to cross some of his polyantha seedlings with 'Tom Thumb' and 'Oakington Ruby'. Because it was thought that miniature roses were infertile, pollen from the miniature varieties was used on larger roses. The first of these seedlings were not considered good eno-ugh to introduce commercially but some were used as parents in his breeding pro-gramme. It was not until 1952 that he intro-duced 'Cutie', the first of the American miniature roses. These first varieties were small with informal flowers. Few are grown today. Improvements were made over the years and by the mid 1960s miniatures like 'Beauty Secret' with true hybrid tea form were being introduced.

It is possible that those first miniatures of the early 1800s may have been selected seedlings of *R. chinensis* and, as such, could even have originated in England or France. It is interesting to find that in the 1960s Ralph Moore grew in three separate years self-set seed from an isolated plant of 'Old Blush' ('Parson's Pink China'), one of the roses which came to Europe in the late eighteenth century. He comments: 'Germ-ination was rather poor. . ., a number of the seedlings were definitely of the miniature type. In seven years, several of these have grown no more than 7 to 12 inches in height.' Perhaps 150 years earlier European growers were getting the same results.

Ralph Moore still hybridizes miniature roses. Over the years he has continued to improve the varieties he has grown and has added to them many strange and novel variations. His 'Stars 'n' Stripes' was one of the first small roses with stripes. 'Fairy Moss', 'Dresden Doll' and others are moss miniatures. More recently he has been working with Rugosa roses to get miniature forms. 'Star Delight' has miniature flowers on a small shrub-like bush. His most recent interest is 'halo' roses, where a lighter halo surrounds the darker centre of the bloom. He is rightly known as the father of the modern miniature rose.

The Americans in particular have taken to the growing of miniature roses with great enthusiasm. In their large rose shows there are as many miniature roses as other types. Nurseries both large and small specialise in the production of miniature rose plants; most have their own breeding programme and more and more varieties are becoming available.

It is not only in North America that new miniature roses are bred, however. They are found wherever roses are grown and many of our new varieties come from the established rose breeders of Britain and Europe, while in New Zealand and Aust-ralia hybridizers like Sam McGredy have a number of varieties to their credit.

Over the years the perception of what a miniature rose should be has changed. The early miniature roses were small; small flowers on small plants. In the 1960s the reviews of newer miniature roses were crit-icizing varieties such as 'Beauty Secret' and 'Baby Darling' as being 'too big for a true miniature rose'. Today, when blooms on new miniature roses seem to be getting ever larger, it is these older varieties that are now considered typical miniature roses.

At some point it becomes necessary to

'Just for You'

say, 'Stop. These blooms and leaves really are too large for a miniature rose.' It happened in England in the 1980s. A group of rose companies, including Dicksons, Harkness and Fryers, had a number of new varieties, bred as miniatures, in which the flowers and foliage were too large to be miniatures but too small and the plant too compact to be a floribunda. They were good attractive varieties but a new name was needed. For whatever reason they became 'patio roses' and the name has stuck and become accepted around the world.

But patio roses as a type did not happen overnight. In England they are regarded as dwarf cluster-flowered roses and English growers were talking about dwarf perpetual-cluster roses back in the early 1900s. These were mainly the dwarf polyantha roses, bred by crossing a dwarf form of *R. multiflora* (sometimes called *R. polyantha*) with a dwarf China rose, possibly *R. chi-*

nensis minima. Some of them are still grown and one has become particularly popular. Often taken for a miniature, 'The Fairy' is actually a polyantha. Another polyantha is 'White Pet', now often grouped with the patio roses.

Over the years these first polyantha roses were crossed with the new hybrid tea roses and became the hybrid polyanthas of the 1930s and 1940s. They often had hybrid tea-type flowers and were usually taller than the older polyanthas. They became our modern floribundas. Many miniature roses and most patio roses have a floribunda as one parent and many patio roses are closer in growth and appearance to a floribunda than to a miniature rose. Because the class 'patio rose' is not recognized by the International Rose Registration Authority, patio roses must be registered as either

'Work of Art'

'Rise 'n' Shine'

miniature or floribunda. A number, such as 'Sweet Dream', 'Rexy's Baby' and 'Patio Jewel', are registered as floribundas and this tells us something about the size of flower and plant. Dwarf floribundas are often sold as patio roses.

Modern miniature roses often have complex parentage and a number are quite fertile and produce copious viable seed. 'Rise 'n' Shine' is a Ralph Moore seedling from 1977. It is one of the best yellow miniature roses ever produced and is still considered the standard against which new yellows are judged. It is also a good parent. It is at least a fourth generation miniature rose. One of its parents was 'Yellow Magic', also bred from a miniature, an unnamed seedling. The other parent was 'Little Darling', a floribunda which figured prominently in Ralph's breeding programme.

From 'Rise 'n' Shine' crossed 'Watercolour' (another miniature rose with 'Little Darling' in its parentage) came 'Rainbow's End'. 'Rainbow's End' has itself been a parent of a number of new miniature roses. When looking at a family tree like this, would-be hybridizers may be tempted to think that if they were to use the same varieties they would get similar results. While this may be a good place to start, the chances of getting another 'Rainbow's End' are very slim. On the other hand something better may just turn up!

Chapter 2

CREATING NEW ROSES

'Si'

Growing roses from seed

NEW varieties of roses are grown from seed. When roses are grown from cuttings or by budding they remain the same as the plant from which the cuttings or buds were taken. Seedling roses may have some of the characteristics of their parents but are frequently completely different. The rose hybridizer has learnt from careful observation which desirable qualities of health, colour or form a variety is likely to carry over to its offspring. By taking the pollen from the stamens of one to sprinkle onto the pistil of another it is hoped to combine the best features of both.

With luck the seed will set, be harvested and sown to germinate and provide a new crop of seedlings, each different and some with the potential to be magnificent. The seedlings are carefully watched and culled

to remove those with a tendency towards disease or uninteresting blooms or colours. The thousands become hundreds for another season's observation; and then tens and finally the few which are considered good enough or different enough to offer for sale.

You can grow roses from seed. The easiest way is to wait until the autumn and collect some ripe hips from your roses. Hips are ripe when they turn orange. Carefully cut the hip open and you will find the seed. Miniature rose hips are small and often have only one or two seeds. This is why many miniature rose breeders use large roses as the seed parent.

If you have been deadheading your roses you may not find many hips. Another year you may decide to leave a few selected blooms to produce hips or you might like

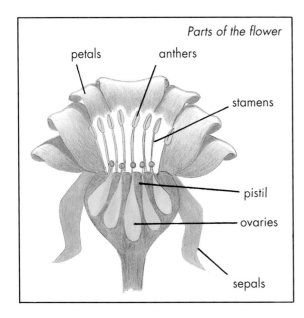

Parts of the flower

petals anthers

stamens

pistil

ovaries

sepals

to try shifting pollen from one bloom to another as the professionals do. This is done in the early summer to give the hips which form time to ripen.

Before the rose chosen to be the seed parent fully opens, remove the petals and stamens to prevent unwanted pollen falling on the pistil. Pollen can be brought to this rose with a small paint brush, a damp finger or by bringing the whole rose head with its stamens intact to brush gently across the prepared pistil.

Remove the seed from the hips, wrap it in some damp absorbent material like a paper towel and put in a plastic bag. Even if you

Rose hips and seed.

can't remember where the pollen came from for your seeds, you do know which plant the hip came from. Later you will want to know what variety produced the best seedlings, so keep different varieties separate and place a tag with the variety name in the bag with the seed. Keep them in a cool place, such as the crisper bin in the refrigerator, over winter.

In the early spring sow the seed in potting mix in a seed tray in the greenhouse or place it in a sheltered spot in the garden. Remember to write the seed parent name on a label placed in the appropriate position. The seed will germinate erratically. Some will grow like weeds; others will not grow at all. If the seedlings are too close together, they may be transplanted into other pots or trays. This is best done when they are very small. Others may be left to grow and flower in the tray where the seed was sown. Do try to keep track of the names of the parent variety.

The seedlings will flower in a few months. At this stage the flowers will be smaller and have fewer petals than they will when the plant matures, but a five-petalled rose will never become full petalled. Most will be single and many will be some shade of pink, as these are the characteristics carried down from the original wild roses in the complex background of your new seedling's parents. You are unlikely to discard as many as a professional would, but don't waste time with plants which become smothered in mildew or some other disease.

It is fun to grow a few plants from seed. You may not be a Ralph Moore or a Sam McGredy but these seedlings are your own and no-one else has another quite like them. Although you don't grow thousands of seedlings, console yourself that it only takes one seed to produce the plant that is the next winner!

New rose varieties also occur naturally by

Ralph Moore inspecting his new seedlings in California.

One of Ralph Moore's 'Halo' seedlings (note its dark red central ring).

a genetic change often called sporting. The most obvious change that can take place as a shoot grows is to produce a flower with a completely different colour. If this happens in your garden, mark the flower by tying a ribbon or tag on the shoot. Leave it to flower again and if it still has the new colour you can try taking this flowering stem as a cutting. If this grows and still retains the new colour you have a new variety of your own. It may be better or worse than the original but it is still considered different. We think more sports occur than is generally realized, for often there may not be something as obvious as a difference in colour but perhaps just a change in vigour, leaf size or the number of petals.

Names

If you get a truly good new rose you will want to give it a name. Call it anything you wish: 'Mother's Choice', 'The Best'. Unless it is going to be widely distributed it is unlikely to cause confusion even if the name already exists. More care needs to be taken if it is a good rose and the name is to be registered. Contact your local rose society for advice about how to do this.

Many books could be written about how roses got their names. Sometimes they are fairly obvious. 'Mary Marshall', 'Luis Desamero' and 'Rose Gilardi' are named after people. 'Beauty Secret', 'Snow Twinkle' and 'Rainbow's End' have something to say about the colour and form of the flower. Others like 'Mother's Love', 'Stolen Dreams', and 'Irresistible' are just good names which seem to fit the variety. Sometimes there are problems. A grower who was endeavouring to register his new rose had sent three names for registration and the first two had been turned down. Now the reply was in for the third and once again it was rejected. The secretary turned to the grower and said, 'We'll just have to call it something else.' And that's what its name became — 'Something Else.'

'Popcorn'

Professional growers often register their new varieties under a trade name which identifies both the raiser and the variety. You will frequently see these names in brackets following the usual variety name. 'Moonlight Lady' has the trade name SOCalp. 'SOC' shows that the raiser is Southern Cross Nurseries, while 'alp' is their code to identify the variety in the nursery. MACnickel is a rose bred by Sam McGredy while MIChome is a variety from Michael Williams. (There are at least three people with the name of Williams breeding roses.)

These trade names are important as rose names may be changed as they go from one country to another, sometimes with unfortunate results. 'Peek A Boo' (DIC-grow) raised in Northern Ireland was renamed 'Brass Ring' when it went to the United States and apparently in Ireland a

brass ring is something you use in a marriage when you don't have a wedding ring. Often for commercial reasons a name is changed to one that is considered to have greater local appeal or to recognise a national celebrity. 'Pandemonium' (MACpandem) is known in England as 'Claire Rayner', where it was introduced as having a 'pandemonium of colour'. Wherever it is grown, the variety still has the trade name, MACpandem.

Good roses from both amateur and professional breeders can be placed on trial for assessment by other growers. Different countries conduct their trials in different ways. The Americans place a variety on trial in a number of different locations and a national award is made to roses which perform well in all areas. Miniature roses receive the AOE, the Award of Excellence of the American Rose Society. Most other countries have awards associated with a particular trial in a particular city. The Royal National Rose Society has its headquarters and display gardens, The Gardens of the Rose, at St Albans and associated with them are their trial grounds. Other trials are conducted in Belfast, Northern Ireland, and in Dublin, Eire. Many European cities have their trial grounds, notable among them are those at The Hague, Holland. In New Zealand, trial grounds exist in Manurewa, Auckland, and in Palmerston North. If you are ever in any of these areas and interested in roses try and visit the trial grounds and see the latest varieties.

Growing roses from cuttings

Producing more plants of an existing rose can be done in several different ways. Miniature roses are usually grown from cuttings. For the home gardener these are best taken in the autumn. Choose a stem which has carried a flower and has at least three true leaves. Remove it from the bush by cutting just below a leaf, leaving three or

four true leaves on the stem and then cut off the top just above a leaf. Take off the bottom leaf and carefully push the cutting two or three centimetres into a free-draining mix in a tray or small pot. Don't bury any leaves. On short cuttings it may be necessary to remove a second leaf. A rooting hormone will help the cutting to root more quickly.

Leave it to grow. Experience has shown that the longer the leaves stay on the cutting, the better it grows. Don't allow the mix to dry out, and try to sprinkle or mist the cutting with water in hot weather. It should be possible to transplant your new plant into the garden or a larger pot in the spring.

It sometimes happens that as miniature rose plants get older, and because they are usually grown from cuttings, the centre of the plant gets woody and the best growth is found around the outside. With care, these plants can be treated like many perennials. Lift them from the ground in the winter and cut into smaller pieces, each with its own root. Discard the old centre portion and plant the others as new rose bushes.

It is possible to multiply miniature and patio roses by budding or grafting. This is done in the same way that larger roses are propagated but is not easy for the home gardener as the buds are so very small. If you want to try this look for instructions in any good book on general rose growing. Standard roses must be grown this way.

Miniature roses can also be grown by micropropagation. This is a laboratory technique where a minute piece of growing tissue is placed under aseptic conditions in a flask containing nutrient solution. Multiplication takes place and by division small plantlets can be produced in great numbers very quickly. This method is not practical for the home gardener and is not frequently used by professional growers. If some genetic change should take place

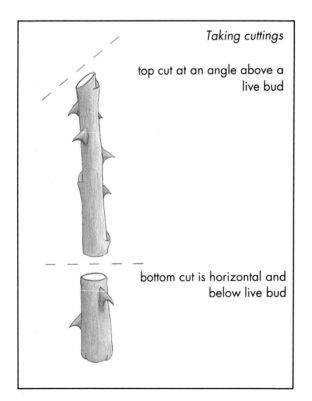

Taking cuttings

top cut at an angle above a live bud

bottom cut is horizontal and below live bud

Above: Miniature roses in the test gardens at the American Rose Society garden in Shreveport, USA.

Right: Miniature roses at the Trial Grounds, Palmerston North, New Zealand.

during the process the grower could finish up with thousands of plants not true to variety.

Miniature roses usually grow easily from cuttings and this is a good way to increase plants for your own garden, but a word of caution must be given. Today most countries have some form of plant protection or patenting, and varieties protected in this way cannot be grown for sale without a licence. Grow them for your own garden but don't grow them for the school fair or to sell at the gate. Many of the popular varieties introduced over the past ten years are protected.

Chapter 3

SOME SELECTED VARIETIES

'Cheers'

A few years ago it would have been possible to include almost all the miniature roses in a book of this type, but in recent years so many new varieties have become available that this is out of the question. The following selected list includes miniature and patio roses both old and new — some for historical reasons and others which may be considered borderline varieties but which in a different time and in a different place could have been called miniature or patio roses.

The list includes roses from a number of the major growing areas throughout the world. Some of these varieties may not currently be available, but they are nevertheless important as they illustrate trends and directions from the past and for the future. Descriptions are largely based upon our experience with the varieties in our garden. Under other conditions and in other climates variations will occur.

Most of the details of parentage and hybridizer are taken from *Modern Roses* 10, The American Rose Society, Shreveport, Louisiana, 1993.

AOE means that the variety received an Award of Excellence of the American Rose Society.

The brackets ( ) enclose the trade name. The name in the [ ] brackets is an alternative name.

Angel Pink (MORgel) This miniature climber has well-shaped flowers of salmon pink with a yellow base to the petals and healthy upright growth. Sometimes a little slow to start climbing, it can eventually reach 2 m grown as a pillar rose.

Parentage: Little Darling x Eleanor
Hybridizer/Year: Moore 1987

'Anytime'

'Baby Faurax'

Angela Rippon (OcaRU) There is no question that this rose gives a great show in the garden and it is probably this which makes it so popular in England. The loosely-petalled salmon pink blooms come in large clusters on a healthy bushy plant.
  Parentage: Rosy Jewel x Zorina
  Hybridizer/Year: de Ruiter 1978

Angelita (MACangeli) [Snowball] This ground-cover miniature is more mounding than trailing. It is a very good rose in the right place. Over the spring and summer it seems to be always covered in small creamy-white-tinged-pink flowers.
  Parentage: Moana x Snow Carpet
  Hybridizer/Year: McGredy 1982

Anytime The flowers are distinctive both because of their fluted petals and informal shape, and because of the dusky orange to pink colouring. Ralph Moore and other prominent hybridizers have been using this variety a lot in their breeding pro-grammes, but it is worth growing for its own merits.
  Parentage: New Penny x Elizabeth of Glamis
  Hybridizer/Year: McGredy 1973

Apricot Medinette *see* Patio Flame

Aoraki (SOCmount) Aoraki is the southern Maori name for Mount Cook, the highest mountain in New Zealand, and loosely translated from the Maori means 'Cloud

Piercer'. The semi-double flowers of this very vigorous miniature climber are white blushed pink. When you see Aoraki in bloom you will be reminded of the early morning sun touching snow.
  Parentage: Jeanne Lajoie seedling
  Hybridizer/Year: Eagle 1994

Baby Faurax This dwarf polyantha rose has small, double, deep violet blooms with some fragrance. The blooms come in large clusters.
  Parentage: unknown
  Hybridizer/Year: Lille 1924

Bay Glow (SOCtepu) Unlike many, this miniature rose remains shorter and is ideal in the front of the garden or in a container. The flowers are large for the size of the plant and are bright yellow with attractive orange/red tonings as they age.
  Parentage: Ferris Wheel seedling
  Hybridizer/Year: Eagle 1992

Beauty Secret Often miniature roses with 'Little Darling' as a parent have pointed petals, and this was one of the first. The medium-red flowers have shapely, pointed buds which pick well. Red roses are always expected to have a scent, and this one will not disappoint you. AOE 1975
  Parentage: Little Darling x Magic Wand
  Hybridizer/Year: Moore 1965

Benson and Hedges Special *see* Dorola

Biddy (BENbid) Although bred in the

'Biddy'

'Brenda Lee'

United States, we understand that this rose has not been released there and they are missing out on a good garden variety. There are masses of informal flowers of deep cream with pink on the outer petals.

Parentage: not given

Hybridizer/Year: Benardella

Black Jade (BENblack) The dark velvety buds are the nearest thing to black ever seen in a rose to date. If left to open in the sun, the colour changes to a medium red. The well-shaped blooms are popular for picking and exhibiting. AOE 1985

Parentage: Sheri Anne x Laguna

Hybridizer/Year: Benardella 1985

Brass Ring *see* Peek a Boo

Brenda Lee (MIClee) We were lucky enough to sit at the same table as Brenda Lee and her husband the evening this variety was launched. It is a true miniature rose, with small well-shaped flowers of yellow with pink to red edges which become more pronounced in full sun. Makes a good edging or pot plant.

Parentage: Rise 'n' Shine x Rainbow's End

Hybridizer/Year: Michael Williams 1991

Café Olé (MORolé) The name says it all. The well-shaped blooms are the colour of milky coffee. They are borne singly and in sprays of three to five, have a spicy fragrance, and are carried on a tall vigorous bush. Unfortunately the colour is variable and, depending on conditions, the flowers may show more lavender grey, like 'Winter Magic'.

Parentage: Winter Magic sport

Hybridizer/Year: Moore 1990

Calumet (SOCapan) Named 'Calumet' (the peace pipe) because of its similarity to 'Peace' in miniature. The lemon-yellow well-shaped flowers are touched with pink on the edges of the petals, and are sometimes paler in hot weather.

Parentage: Golden Angel seedling

Hybridizer/Year: Eagle 1985

Candy Cane An early climbing miniature with flowers of deep pink striped pale pink. They come in loose clusters on a vigorous, open, climbing plant.

Parentage: Seedling x Zee

Hybridizer/Year: Moore 1958

'Candy Cane'

'Chick-a-Dee'

Chasin' Rainbows (SAVachase) A miniature version of 'Rainbow's End', with yellow flowers edged with bright red on a small compact plant.

  Parentage: Zorina x Rainbow's End
  Hybridizer/Year: Saville 1988

Cheers (SAValot) This miniature rose has a most unusual colour combination. The well-shaped flowers are burnt orange with a lighter reverse, and will deepen to almost brown in cooler weather.

  Parentage: Poker Chip x Zinger
  Hybridizer/Year: Saville 1984

Chelsea (MORsea) The small medium-pink double blooms with lacy sepals are borne in clusters on a compact plant. The first miniature rose with sepals like 'Crested Moss'.

  Parentage: (Little Darling x Yellow Magic) x Crested Jewel
  Hybridizer/Year: Moore 1986

Chick-a-Dee (MORchick) We saw this variety first at Ralph Moore's nursery in California and were impressed by the amount of bloom even on tiny plants. The flowers are light pink with occasional paler stripes on a short compact plant. An ideal garden rose.

  Parentage: Cecile Brunner x (Dortmund x (Fairy Moss x (Little Darling x Ferdinand Pichard))
  Hybridizer/Year: Moore 1990

Cider Cup (DICladida) The well-formed flowers are a deep apricot blend, and have a slight fragrance. They are borne singly and in small sprays on a bushy plant, and are the typically larger size of an English patio rose.

  Parentage: Memento x (Liverpool Echo x Woman's Own)
  Hybridizer/Year: Dickson 1988

Claire Rayner see Pandemonium

Clarissa (HARprocrustes) Taller and more slender than some patio roses, 'Clarissa' has well-formed blooms of yellow apricot in large clusters. The foliage is dark and glossy. It won the Gold Star of the South Pacific at the New Zealand Trial Grounds.

  Parentage: Southampton x Darling Flame
  Hybridizer/Year: Harkness 1983

Cream Puff A patio rose from Dee Bennett, the semi-double flowers are cream blushed with pink, and are at their best when fully open. The blooms come singly or in small clusters.

  Parentage: Little Darling x Elfinesque
  Hybridizer/Year: Bennett 1981

Crimson Medinette *see* Patio Prince

'Cream Puff'

'Debut'

Cupcake (SPIcup) The clear medium-pink flowers are well shaped, high centred, and have reflexing petals. The colour holds well both on the bush and when picked. AOE 1983

    Parentage: Gene Boerner x (Gay Princess x Yellow Jewel)

    Hybridizer/Year: Spies 1981

Dainty Dinah (COCamond) The orange/pink to red blooms of this patio rose are well formed and very prolific.

    Parentage: Anne Cocker x Wee Man

    Hybridizer/Year: Cocker 1981

Debidue (MICdeb) A true miniature rose. The deep pink to magenta blooms are quite small and come mainly one to a stem. AOE 1992.

    Parentage: Jazz Fest x Party Girl

    Hybridizer/Year: Michael Williams 1992

Debut (MEIbarke) [Sweet Symphony] This is a bright and showy miniature rose with semi-double flowers of a luminous scarlet blending to deep cream at the base. It makes a bushy plant, wider than it is tall. 'Debut' was one of the first varieties to receive an All American Rose Selection award when miniatures became eligible in 1989.

    Parentage: Coppelia x Magic Carrousel

    Hybridizer/Year: Selection Meilland 1989

Deep Velvet The shapely dark red blooms come singly or in small clusters and are ideal for picking.

    Parentage: (Grand Opera x Jimmy Greaves) x Baby Katie

    Hybridizer/Year: Jolly 1981

Dorola (MACshana) [Benson and Hedges Special] This is one of the taller patio roses, with large unfading bright yellow blooms. The nicely shaped buds are ideal for picking.

    Parentage: Darling Flame x Mabella

    Hybridizer/Year: McGredy 1982

Dreamglo This vigorous bush stands out in the garden. The flowers are a brilliant red with white at the base of the petals and are of good exhibition form.

    Parentage: Little Darling x Little Chief

    Hybridizer/Year: E.D. Williams 1978

'Dreamglo'

'Explorer's Dream'

Dresden Doll One of the better moss miniatures from Ralph Moore. The stems and sepals are very mossy, and the delicate pink blooms look like Dresden china.
    Parentage: Fairy Moss x Moss seedling
    Hybridizer/Year: Moore 1975
Drummer Boy (HARvacity) In England in the summer of 1991 this patio rose attracted our attention. Clusters of vivid bright scarlet semi-double flowers covered the spreading plants, which seemed to be completely disease free.
    Parentage: (Wee Man x (Southampton x Darling Flame)) x Red Sprite
    Hybridizer/Year: Harkness 1987
Explorer's Dream (MICexplore) The flowers are a deep orange/pink with just a touch of yellow at the base of each petal. The blooms are borne in small clusters and have excellent form.
    Parentage: seedling x Homecoming
    Hybridizer/Year: Michael Williams 1992
Fairhope (TALfairhope) This miniature rose from a new breeder has risen rapidly to become a popular exhibition bloom in the United States. The soft pastel cream flowers are a good shape and normally come one to a stem.
    Parentage: Azure Sea x seedling
    Hybridizer/Year: Taylor 1989
Ferdy (KEItoli) The deep coral pink small flowers come in profusion on a spreading,

sprawling plant. Don't grow this for the individual flowers, but for the mass of colour during late spring and early summer. Unfortunately it does not repeat flower well.
    Parentage: Climbing seedling x Petite Folie seedling
    Hybridizer/Year: Suzuki 1984
Figurine (BENfig) The very pale pink flowers usually come in small clusters. The buds are long and are good for picking. AOE 1992
    Parentage: Rise 'n' Shine x Laguna
    Hybridizer/Year: Benardella 1992
Flower Carpet (NOAtraum) The deep cerise pink informal flowers come on a vigorous spreading bush which has turned out to be much taller and wider than expected.
    Parentage: Immensee x Amanda
    Hybridizer/Year: Noack 1991
Fresh Pink (MACpinderal) A miniature rose described by the name. The colour is great. The buds are attractive and the semi-double flowers best when they are fully open.
    Parentage: not given
    Hybridizer/Year: McGredy 1987

'Figurine'

Gentle Touch (DIClulu) The soft pink flowers look good in the garden on a well-proportioned plant. They also pick well. This patio rose is attractive in a container.
 Parentage: (Liverpool Echo x Woman's Own) x Memento
 Hybridizer/Year: Dickson 1986
Glowing Carpet *see* Ralph's Creeper
Golden Gardens (MORgoguard) This is a

'Golden Gardens'

taller miniature rose, and could be grown as a shrub rose or as a short climber. The many informal blooms are a bright medium yellow.
 Parentage: (Little Darling x Yellow Magic) x Gold Badge
 Hybridizer/Year: Moore 1988

Golden Song The flowers of this miniature climber are particularly showy against a dark background. They are golden yellow with orange/red highlights. The long pointed buds open to well-shaped hybrid tea-type blooms.

Parentage: Little Darling x Golden Angel
Hybridizer/Year: E.D. Williams 1980

Golden Sunblaze *see* Rise 'n' Shine

Gourmet Popcorn (WEOpop) Abundant small buds and fragrant white blooms in large clusters cover this vigorous plant. Its mass of flower and healthy dark green foliage make it ideal for the garden.

Parentage: Popcorn sport
Hybridizer/Year: Desamero 1986

Green Ice The flowers and growth habit of this variety are more like those of a short polyantha than a miniature rose. Its buds first show a touch of pink and change to creamy white with a hint of soft green as they open. Grown in semi-shade, the green will be more pronounced. The spreading habit makes it an ideal container or hanging basket plant.

Parentage: (*R. wichuraiana* x Floradora) x Jet Trail
Hybridizer/Year: Moore 1971

Heart 'n' Soul (LAVsans) [Sans Souci] The well-formed flowers of this miniature rose are a deep cerise pink and are borne in profusion on a bushy plant which repeats quickly.

Parentage: Rise 'n' Shine x Ontario Celebration
Hybridizer/Year: Laver 1986

High Spirits (SAVaspri) This variety deserves more attention than it gets, particularly as a garden rose. The long-lasting bright red flowers come in sprays on a vigorous, healthy, upright plant.

Parentage: Sheri Anne x Tamango
Hybridizer/Year: Saville 1983

Hurdy Gurdy (MACpluto) This patio rose can't make up its mind whether it is a tall bush or a short climber. The flowers have

'Indian Summer'

pronounced crimson and white stripes and are a good shape.

Parentage: Matangi x Stars 'n' Stripes
Hybridizer/Year: McGredy 1986

Indian Summer (HARwigwam) A patio climber or pillar rose. It has well-shaped flowers of a soft pinky-apricot/orange blend which come in small clusters. Ideal for picking as well as a garden plant. Growth is vigorous and healthy.

Parentage: Liverpool Echo x Bobby Dazzler
Hybridizer/Year: Harkness 1991

Irresistible (TINresist) The many-petalled well-formed flowers are near white with a deeper centre. They have a slightly spicy fragrance and are usually borne singly and in small sprays. The high-centred blooms and long-lasting qualities make this an ideal picking and exhibition rose.

Parentage: Tiki x Brian Lee
Hybridizer/Year: Bennett 1990

Jean Kenneally (TINeally) This rose climbed rapidly up the list of favourite miniature roses of the New Zealand National Rose Society. This is not surprising, as for several years it has been the top or among the top exhibition miniature roses in the United States. The well-formed buds and flowers are an unfading pink/apricot on a tall, vigorous bush. 'Jean Kenneally' needs a year in the garden to reach its full potential. AOE 1986

Parentage: Futura x Party Girl
Hybridizer/Year: Bennett 1984

Jeanne Lajoie An excellent vigorous climbing miniature rose. 'Jeanne Lajoie' grows strongly and covers itself with small well-formed buds and double flowers of a lovely medium rose pink. AOE 1977

Parentage: (Casa Blanca x Independence) x Midget
Hybridizer/Year: Sima 1975

Jennifer (BENjen) The porcelain-like flowers of pale lavender-pink have a silver reverse. The buds are an excellent shape, and the petals stand up well in inclement weather. AOE 1985

Parentage: Party Girl x Laguna
Hybridizer/Year: Benardella 1985

Jewel Box (MORbox) With 'Old Master' as a parent, this miniature rose shows the handpainted effect in its mauve/pink and white colouring. The colours and markings

'Jennifer'

'Jim Dandy'

become more defined in hot weather. It gives abundant bloom on a neat bushy plant.

Parentage: Avandel x Old Master
Hybridizer/Year: Moore 1984

Jim Dandy (BENjim) The pointed buds and flowers are a medium red with yellow reverse. The flowers are high centred and borne singly or in small sprays. AOE 1989

Parentage: Rise 'n' Shine x Marina
Hybridizer/Year: Benardella 1988

Just For You (MORyou) The well-formed flowers of this miniature rose are dark pink to light red in colour, with a lighter reverse. AOE 1991

Parentage: Orangeade x Rainbow's End
Hybridizer/Year: Moore 1990

Kaikoura (MACwalla) A popular patio rose in New Zealand, 'Kaikoura' often wins at rose shows with its glowing orange/red larger flowers. The plant is vigorous, healthy and free blooming.

Parentage: Anytime x Matangi
Hybridizer/Year: McGredy 1978

Kapiti (MACglemil) This ground-cover/shrub rose covers itself in bright pink patio-sized flowers with prominent

'Kapiti'

'Lemon Twist'

stamens. The fluted petals are inherited from 'Anytime' which was a grandparent of 'Sexy Rexy'. On its own roots it establishes quickly and forms a compact, spreading plant.

    Parentage: Sexy Rexy x Eyeopener

    Hybridizer/Year: McGredy 1992

Kent (POUlcov) [Sparkler] One of the popular English County series, 'Kent' has white semi-double flowers in large trusses on a spreading, shrubby plant. The flowers are unaffected by rain.

    Parentage: not given

    Hybridizer/Year: Olesen 1988

Laura Ford (CHEwarvel) An upright patio climber with flowers of medium yellow showing a pink flush with age. The foliage is dark green and glossy.

    Parentage: Anna Ford x (Elizabeth of Glamis x (Galway Bay x Sutter's Gold))

    Hybridizer/Year: Warner 1990

Lemon Twist (FOUtwist) The lemon-

yellow flowers are unfading and of good shape. They come mainly one to a stem and are good for picking and in the garden.

    Parentage: Gold Badge x Great Day

    Hybridizer/Year: Jacobs 1988

Little Girl One of the most popular climbing miniature roses. The deep coral pink flowers have an attractive bud and are useful for picking. The practically thornless, tall, pillar-type plant has dark green glossy foliage.

    Parentage: Little Darling x Westmont

    Hybridizer/Year: Moore 1973

Little Jackie (SAVor) The miniature hybrid-tea-shaped flowers are salmon/orange with yellow reverse. The plant is tall and the flowers come on long stems and are ideal for picking and exhibiting. AOE 1984

    Parentage: (Prominent x Sheri Anne) x Glenfiddich

    Hybridizer/Year: Saville 1982

Little Nugget (SUNgold) Unfading golden-yellow flowers of good form that keep well. Plants produce an abundance of flowers with a good stem length for picking.

    Parentage: Lorena x Firefly

    Hybridizer/Year: Schuurman 1991

Little Opal (SUNpat) The light pink flowers are a good hybrid tea shape. In warm areas this is a patio rose, but in cooler conditions the flowers can become as large as many floribundas.

    Parentage: White Dream x Dicky Bird

    Hybridizer/Year: Schuurman 1991

Little Showoff This miniature climber has golden-yellow flowers with prominent orange overtones. The plant is open and spreading.

    Parentage: Golden Glow x Zee

    Hybridizer/Year: Moore 1960

Little White Pet *see* White Pet

Little Woman (DIClittle) The flowers of this patio rose are an apricot-pink blend and a good hybrid tea shape.

    Parentage: Memento x (Liverpool Echo x Woman's Own)

    Hybridizer/Year: Dickson, 1986

'Little Showoff'

'Lucky Me'

Loving Touch This free-flowering bushy patio rose has long elegant buds of true apricot which open to blooms of buff apricot. The blooms come singly or in small clusters, and are ideal for picking. AOE 1985

    Parentage: Rise 'n' Shine x First Prize

    Hybridizer/Year: Jolly 1982

Lucky Me (SOCluck) Several years ago we entered one of the first flowers of this variety in a local rose show. It won first prize in its class. Lucky me! The many-petalled flowers are a deep rose pink, and are of hybrid tea shape. They come in abundance on a disease-resistant, bushy patio plant.

    Parentage: Heidi seedling

    Hybridizer/Year: Eagle 1993

Luis Desamero (TINluis) Named for an outstanding exhibitor from California, this patio rose has pale lemon flowers which can be quite large. They have good form and are popular with exhibitors in the United States. The bushes are tall and healthy.

    Parentage: Tiki x Baby Katie

    Hybridizer/Year: Bennett 1989

Magic Carrousel (MORrousel) Popular for many years, this bicolour miniature is white with a deep pink edging to the petals. The flowers are displayed best when fully open. The bushes are upright and can grow very tall. AOE 1975.

Parentage: Little Darling x Westmont
Hybridizer/Year: Moore 1972

Magic Dragon One of the few deep red climbing miniature roses. The flowers are semi-double and open flat, making a good display on a vigorous upright plant.

Parentage: ((*R. wichuraiana* x Floradora) x seedling) x Little Buckaroo
Hybridizer/Year: Moore 1969

Make Believe (MORmake) The semi-double blooms begin as red/purple buds and open to show a lighter centre with prominent yellow stamens. The flowers usually come in small clusters.

Parentage: Anytime x Angel Face
Hybridizer/Year: Moore 1986

Mary Marshall One of the older miniature roses and named after an outstanding Californian rosarian. The attractive blooms are coral orange with a yellow base to the petals. Still well worth growing. AOE 1975

Parentage: Little Darling x Fairy Princess
Hybridizer/Year: Moore 1970

Minnie Pearl (SAVahowdy) If this miniature rose has a fault it is that the flowers can vary in colour. When grown in the shade or under cover they may be very pale pink. As the amount of sun increases the colour intensifies to a deeper pink with yellow tonings. The buds and blooms are of excellent form and are popular for picking and for exhibiting. The bush is tall and vigorous.

Parentage: (Little Darling x Tiki) x Party Girl
Hybridizer/Year: Saville 1982

Moonlight Lady (SOCalp) We are very proud of this miniature rose. The flowers have excellent exhibition form and win consistently at rose shows. The many,

'Mary Marshall'

petalled blooms are creamy white softly touched with pastel pink/buff in the centre as the flower opens and come mainly one to a stem. Once established, the plant is tall and vigorous. Its only blemish is the thorns!

Parentage: Pink Petticoat seedling
Hybridizer/Year: Eagle 1987

Mother's Love (TINlove) This patio rose is a little similar to 'Jean Kenneally', which has the same parentage. The flowers are salmon pink with attractive buds. It is constantly in flower. A great name for a rose any mother would love.

Parentage: Futura x Party Girl
Hybridizer/Year: Bennett 1989

Mountie (LAVcale) If you are looking for a bright red rose for a container, this may be it. The flowers and buds are shapely and plentiful.

Parentage: Party Girl x Dwarfking '78
Hybridizer/Year: Laver 1984

'Moonlight Lady'

'My Sunshine'

'Nozomi'

My Sunshine (TINshine) This variety makes a bushy compact plant which covers itself with single blooms of brilliant shining yellow. As the blooms age, they become a pumpkin shade. Some find this attractive as it reminds them of a potentilla.

Parentage: Sunsprite x Fool's Gold
Hybridizer/Year: Bennett 1986

New Beginning (SAVabeg) The very double flowers are a bright orange/yellow bicolour and usually come in small clusters. One of the first miniature roses to receive the All American Rose Selection award in 1989.

Parentage: Zorina x seedling
Hybridizer/Year: Saville 1989

New Fashion *see* Patio Princess

Nice Day *see* Patio Queen

Nickelodeon (MACnickel) Another hand-painted miniature rose which makes a bright splash of colour in the garden. The flowers are semi-double and deep red and white in colour.

Parentage: Roller Coaster x (Freude x ((Anytime x Eyepaint) x Stars 'n' Stripes))
Hybridizer/Year: McGredy 1991

Noelle Marie (SOCnoma) A good garden miniature with attractive buds of creamy apricot opening to blooms of white edged with pale pink. Disease-resistant foliage on a bushy plant.

Parentage: Pink Petticoat seedling
Hybridizer/Year: Eagle 1990

Nozomi This miniature ground-cover rose appeared at a time when most people had never heard of them. It puts out long runners and can quickly cover an area 2 m across. The flowers which smother the plant in the spring and early summer are small, single and pale pink with a touch of creamy white at their centre.

Parentage: Fairy Princess x Sweet Fairy
Hybridizer/Year: Onodera 1968

Old Glory (BENday) The larger miniature blooms are well shaped and a dusky medium red. They are usually borne singly or in small sprays and come on sturdy straight stems. AOE 1988

Parentage: Rise 'n' Shine x Harmonie
Hybridizer/Year: Benardella 1988

Pacesetter (SAVapace) The long, pointed buds of this miniature rose open to pure white flowers with an attractive shape. The plant is tall and upright. One of the best

'Palmetto Sunrise'

'Paquerette'

white roses for picking and cut flowers.
AOE 1981

  Parentage: Ma Perkins x Magic Carrousel
  Hybridizer/Year: Schwartz 1979

Palmetto Sunrise (MICpal) The well-shaped blooms are bright orange-red with a yellow reverse and sometimes show a hint of bronze. A vigorous plant with healthy disease-resistant foliage. AOE 1993

  Parentage: Orange Honey x miniature seedling
  Hybridizer/Year: Michael Williams 1993

Panache (SOCpan) This sport of 'Sachet' is similar in every way but the colour, which is strikingly different. Difficult to describe, it is a soft peach with an occasional suspicion of lavender and tan colourings. It retains the very strong perfume of 'Sachet'.

  Parentage: Sachet sport
  Hybridizer/Year: Eagle 1995

Pandemonium (MACpandem) [Claire Rayner] This bright yellow and orange striped rose is unusual and striking in the garden. 'Pandemonium' looks good with other yellow, orange or red miniatures.

  Parentage: New Year x ((Anytime x Eyepaint) x Stars 'n' Stripes)
  Hybridizer/Year: McGredy 1988

Paquerette Regarded as the first of the polyantha roses, the very double flowers are pure white and carried in large clusters.

  Parentage: uncertain
  Hybridizer/Year: Guillot Fils 1875

Party Girl (SAVapart) This miniature rose has high-centred blooms of a soft apricot yellow flushed salmon pink. Although the flowers have fewer petals than some varieties, they last well both on the plant and when picked. AOE 1981

Parentage: Rise 'n' Shine x Sheri Anne
Hybridizer/Year: Saville 1979

Patio Flame (POUlcot) [Apricot Medinette] The bright apricot/orange well-shaped flowers are borne on a tall, vigorous bush which can be trained as a short climber.

  Parentage: Mini-Poul x Mary Sumner
  Hybridizer/Year: Olesen 1985

'Patio Flame'

'Patio Queen'

'Pierrine'

Patio Prince (POUlcrim) [Crimson Medinette] The velvety dark red blooms are shapely and come mainly in clusters. It holds its colour well from bud to fully open. The plant is healthy, vigorous and taller than average.

Parentage: Seedling x Pygmae
Hybridizer/Year: Olesen 1984

Patio Princess (POUlholm) [New Fashion] The semi-double blooms of this patio climber are a soft apricot/orange. They are at their best when fully open. The plant is tall and vigorous.

Parentage: Mary Sumner x seedling
Hybridizer/Year: Olesen 1989

Patio Queen CHEwsea) [Nice Day] Shapely many-petalled blooms of light salmon pink blend are highlighted against the deep green leaves on this patio climber. The plant is very vigorous and grows quickly.

Parentage: Seaspray x Warm Welcome
Hybridizer/Year: Warner 1993

Peek a Boo (DICgrow) [Brass Ring] Although sometimes considered a patio rose, the flowers and foliage are small and the size of a miniature. The small semi-double flowers come in large clusters and are a light coppery orange which fades as they age.

Parentage: Memento x Nozomi
Hybridizer/Year: Dickson 1981

Peon *see* Tom Thumb

Petticoat Lane (SOCamp) This sister seedling to 'Moonlight Lady' has well-formed medium pink flowers on a healthy vigorous plant.

Parentage: Pink Petticoat seedling
Hybridizer/Year: Eagle 1985

Pierrine (MICpie) A beautiful medium pink very double rose that opens slowly and holds its form and substance for a long time. Excellent for showing, arranging and the garden.

Parentage: Tiki x Party Girl
Hybridizer/Year: Michael Williams 1988

Pink Bells (POUlbells) Strictly speaking not a miniature or a patio rose, but rather a vigorous ground-cover shrub. The large spreading plant is covered with small very double informal flowers of deep pink with fine foliage. The main flowering flush is in late spring and early summer. It makes an excellent weeping standard. 'Red Bells' and 'White Bells' are two other varieties by the same hybridizer, with the same parentage and similar habit of growth.

Parentage: Mini-Poul x Temple Bells
Hybridizer/Year: Poulsen 1983

Pink Petticoat The beautiful shapely blooms of this tall patio rose are creamy white brushed with deep coral pink along the outer edges. They often come in large candelabra heads which have individual

stems long enough to pick. AOE 1980

Parentage: Neue Revue x Sheri Anne
Hybridizer/Year: Strawn 1979

Pink Porcelain (TINporce) The well-shaped flowers are a pale pink and the petals have a good texture, remaining unmarked by the rain — unusual on roses of this colour. The flowers come one to three on a stem, and are ideal for picking.

Parentage: Futura x Avandel
Hybridizer/Year: Bennett 1983

Pink Symphony *see* Pretty Polly

Popcorn The fragrant semi-double tiny white flowers with gold stamens are borne in clusters, making the plant appear to be covered in popcorn. The healthy free-flowering plant has fine fern-like foliage.

Parentage: Katharina Zeimet x Diamond Jewel
Hybridizer/Year: Morey 1973

Pretty Polly (MEItonje) [Pink Symphony] This attractive bushy patio rose has many soft pink double blooms which come mainly in small clusters. It does well in a container and in the garden.

Parentage: Darling Flame x Air France
Hybridizer/Year: Meilland 1987

Pride 'n' Joy (JACmo) The well-formed, bright orange blooms are carried on a spreading bush. All American Rose Selection 1992.

Parentage: Chattem Centennial x Prominent
Hybridizer/Year: Warriner 1992

Radiant (BENrad) This miniature rose can be treated as a short climber or pillar rose. The flowers are orange/red and have a good shape.

Parentage: Sheri Anne x Sheri Anne
Hybridizer/Year: Benardella 1987

Ragtime (MACcourlod) Each of the flowers of this handpainted miniature rose has different markings. They are mostly in bright reds and pinks, some being somewhat paler.

Parentage: Mary Sumner x seedling

'Pride 'n' Joy'

Hybridizer/Year: McGredy 1982

Rainbow's End (SAValife) This is a plant for a bright sunny position. The well-shaped blooms of bright yellow lose the scarlet edge when grown in the shade. The plant is compact and vigorous, with many flowers, and is quick to repeat. AOE 1986

Parentage: Rise 'n' Shine x Watercolor
Hybridizer/Year: Saville 1984

'Ragtime'

'Ralph's Creeper'

'Rise 'n' Shine'

Ralph's Creeper (MORpapplay) [Glowing Carpet] The informal flowers come in large clusters and are a bright red with a yellow eye, showing a paler yellow on the reverse of the petals. The bush is very vigorous with low, spreading growth. If pegged down it gives the effect of a ground cover and will spread over a large area.

  Parentage: Papoose x Playboy
  Hybridizer/Year: Moore 1987

Rexy's Baby (MACcarib) The blooms of this patio rose are pale pink with irregular markings of a paler colour. The very double flowers reflex well and come mainly in small sprays.

  Parentage: Sexy Rexy x (Freude x
  ((Anytime x Eyepaint) x Stars 'n' Stripes))
  Hybridizer/Year: McGredy 1992

Ring of Fire (MORfire) The name has been well chosen for this variety, with its flowers of rich yellow edged with deep orange which look so bright all through the summer. This is an excellent garden variety. AOE 1987

  Parentage: Pink Petticoat x Gold Badge
  Hybridizer/Year: Moore 1986

Rise 'n' Shine [Golden Sunblaze] This brilliant clear yellow miniature rose has many shapely blooms on a superior bush. The blooms are comparatively unfading and repeat quickly. This is still the rose with which all new yellow miniatures are compared. AOE 1978

  Parentage: Little Darling x Yellow Magic
  Hybridizer/Year: Moore 1977

R. chinensis minima This name covers a group of small China roses. The small flowers may be white, pink or red. In cultivation before 1815.

R. rouletti Around the world we have seen a number of roses bearing this name. They all have small informal pink flowers on a short plant, but there have been slight variations in the colour and other small details. One of the early original miniature roses from which many of the newer varieties can trace their parentage.

'Rose Gilardi'

Rose Gilardi (MORose) Deep pink and red stripes make these semi-double mossy flowers unusual. The blooms come in small clusters and are striking without the stridency of some of the earlier striped varieties.

Parentage: Dortmund x ((Fairy Moss x (Little Darling x Ferdinand Pichard)) x seedling)

Hybridizer/Year: Moore 1986

Rosie (BENros) The small flowers are pink with cream reverse and are well shaped. They are good in the garden or for picking.

Parentage: Rise 'n' Shine x (Sheri Anne x Laguna)

Hybridizer/Year: Benardella 1987

Rosy Dawn The healthy plant carries many flowers of creamy yellow edged with deep carmine pink. It is an excellent garden rose, with the brightly coloured flowers attracting much attention.

Parentage: Magic Carrousel seedling

Hybridizer/Year: Bennett 1982

Sachet (SAVasach) A strongly perfumed miniature rose. The loosely-formed dusky lavender blooms are at their best when fully open and the stamens are prominent. They have a heavy damask fragrance, particularly in warm weather.

Parentage: Seedling x Shocking Blue

Hybridizer/Year: Saville 1986

San Jose Sunshine (FOUsun) The well-formed buds open to shapely flowers of deep golden yellow with orange highlights. The plant is vigorous and very floriferous. The official rose of the 1991 American Rose Society Spring Convention in San Jose.

Parentage: (Rise 'n' Shine x Redgold) x Summer Madness

Hybridizer/Year: Jacobs 1991

Sea Foam This patio ground-cover shrub has informal pink to creamy white flowers on a semi-prostrate arching plant.

Parentage: ((White Dawn x Pinocchio) x

'Rosy Dawn'

(White Dawn x Pinocchio)) x (White Dawn x Pinocchio)

Hybridizer/Year: Schwartz 1964

Sequoia Gold (MORsegold) The medium-yellow double flowers, usually in clusters, cover the spreading bushy plants and make it an ideal variety for colour in the garden. Like all yellows, it can fade a little in the heat of the summer as the flowers age. AOE 1987

Parentage: (Little Darling x Lemon Delight) x Gold Badge

Hybridizer/Year: Moore 1986

Si Pedro Dot of Spain was one of the early hybridizers of miniature roses and this is his smallest, and probably the smallest rose in commercial production anywhere in the world. The tiny pink buds are no larger than a grain of wheat and open to

'Sequoia Gold'

'Snow Twinkle'

'Stolen Dream'

semi-double light pink flowers about 1 cm across. The fine foliage and short plant are on a scale to match the flowers.

Parentage: Perla de Montserrat x (Anny x Tom Thumb)

Hybridizer/Year: Dot 1957

Silver (SOCsil) The soft silver lavender flowers have good hybrid tea form and a subtle fragrance. They come one to a stem and in small clusters on a healthy bushy plant.

Parentage: Winsome seedling

Hybridizer/Year: Eagle 1994

Snow Twinkle (MORsno) A good white miniature rose with enough petals to hold the shape well on the bush or when picked. A compact disease-resistant plant which is good in a container or the garden.

Parentage: (Little Darling x Yellow Magic) x Magic Carrousel

Hybridizer/Year: Moore 1987

Snowball *see* Angelita

Sparkler *see* Kent

Stacey Sue Small double informal flowers of soft pink come in clusters and cover the short plant.

Parentage: Ellen Poulsen x Fairy Princess

Hybridizer/Year: Moore 1976

Star Delight (MORstar) [Starry Eyed] Not a miniature, but a modern Rugosa shrub with miniature-sized flowers. The small rose-pink single flowers have white cen-

tres and are borne all along the arching stems in sprays. A hardy shrub for tough situations.

Parentage: Yellow Jewel x Rugosa Magnifica

Hybridizer/Year: Moore 1989

Starina This is a classical miniature rose with a deserved record of popularity in Europe, the United States and New Zealand. The shapely flowers of orange red are borne singly or several together on a healthy vigorous plant.

Parentage: (Dany Robin x Fire King) x Perla de Montserrat

Hybridizer/Year: Meilland 1965

Stolen Dream (MICsteal) There is a profusion of medium to deep pink hybrid-tea type blooms on a vigorous upright bush. The blooms become more of a hot pink in summer and somewhat magenta in cooler weather.

Parentage: not given

Hybridizer/Year: Michael Williams 1995

Sugar 'n' Spice (TINspice) Another patio rose from the late Dee Bennett and, like some other varieties of hers, it makes a magnificent plant once established. The well-formed blooms are a pale peach/apricot pink and last well when cut.

Parentage: Futura x Avandel

Hybridizer/Year: Bennett 1985

Suma (HARsuma) This miniature ground-cover rose has arching growth covered with small full flowers of deep pink to red.

Parentage: Nozomi seedling

Hybridizer/Year: Onodera 1987

Sweet Chariot (MORchari) Plant one or two of these wherever you want perfume in the garden. You won't need to bend to smell the roses as this is one of the most strongly perfumed varieties we know. The flowers are a deep lavender purple and are carried in large clusters on a healthy spreading bush. Good in a container or the garden.

Parentage: Little Chief x Violette

Hybridizer/Year: Moore 1984

Sweet Dream (FRYminicot) The informal blooms of this patio rose are a soft peachy-apricot and come in short-stemmed clusters. Described as small and bushy in England, it can grow much larger in Australia and New Zealand.

Parentage: seedling x seedling

Hybridizer/Year: Fryer 1988

Sweet Magic (DICmagic) This is another typical rose from Pat Dickson, Northern Ireland. The semi-double orange flowers with golden highlights open flat to show prominent stamens.

Parentage: Peek a Boo x Bright Smile

Hybridizer/Year: Dickson 1986

Sweet Symphony *see* Debut

Swinger While officially classed as a miniature, under temperate conditions it becomes almost a floribunda. The well-formed bright golden yellow flowers are large and usually come one to a stem. A good rose in the garden.

Parentage: Anita Charles x Orange Honey

Hybridizer/Year: Jolly 1984

The Fairy Not really a miniature rose but often included with them, 'The Fairy' is a polyantha with typical foliage and rosette blooms. The clear pink flowers come in very large trusses on a vigorous spreading plant. For many years this variety was considered to be a sport of the rambler 'Lady

'Tom Thumb'

Godiva'. A member of the Bentall family has corrected this to the parentage shown.

Parentage: Paul Crampel x Lady Gay

Hybridizer/Year: Bentall 1932

Tigris (HARprier) This variety is a real breakthrough in rose breeding. The small flowers are yellow with a red eye. The foliage is small and in proportion to the flowers, and the stems have gooseberry-like prickles. Before this, flowers had only pale centres of white or yellow, and hybridizers worldwide are hoping to use this variety to expand their colour combinations.

Parentage: Hulthemia persica x Trier

Hybridizer/Year: Harkness 1985

Tom Thumb [Peon] Very small flowers of deep crimson with white centres. One of the first miniature roses.

Parentage: Rouletti x Gloria Mundi

Hybridizer/Year: de Vink 1936

Tracey Wickham Named after a well-known Australian swimmer, this Australian-bred miniature rose has yellow flowers edged with a bright orange/red. The flowers have a good shape and pick well.

Parentage: Avandel x Redgold

Hybridizer/Year: Welsh 1984

Warm Welcome (CHEwizz) Winner of the Gold Medal and President's International Trophy at the Royal National Rose Society in 1988, this climber has patio-sized

'Why Not'

'Wee Jock'

flowers of bright orange vermilion. This pillar rose continually covers itself with blooms from top to bottom throughout the flowering season.

   Parentage: Elizabeth of Glamis x (Galway Bay x Sutter's Gold)) x Anna Ford
   Hybridizer/Year: Warner 1991

Wee Jock (COCabest) The flowers are of bright red with a good shape, useful for the garden or for picking. The vigorous patio plant is bushy and healthy.

   Parentage: National Trust x Wee Man
   Hybridizer/Year: Cocker 1980

White Pet [Little White Pet] A very early dwarf polyantha rose, with pink buds opening to very full white flowers in large clusters on a small bush.

   Parentage: unknown
   Hybridizer/Year: Henderson 1879

Whiteout (MACwhitout) The small rosette-shaped flowers come in clusters covering the compact healthy plant. The buds are a

pale pink, particularly in cool weather, and the open flower is pale pink to white. We find this plant to be very fragrant in warm temperatures. It looks good in the garden or in a container.

   Parentage: Sexy Rexy x Popcorn
   Hybridizer/Year: McGredy 1988

Why Not (MORwhy) The small single flowers are bright red with a prominent yellow eye. When the hybridizer asked a visitor if he should release this rose the visitor replied 'Why Not?' and that is how this variety was named.

   Parentage: Golden Angel x seedling
   Hybridizer/Year: Moore 1983

Winter Magic (FOUmagic) People either love or loathe this miniature rose because of its unusual colour. The long shapely buds and flowers are lavender grey and very fragrant. The plant is upright and the flowers last well when picked.

   Parentage: Rise 'n' Shine x Blue Nile
   Hybridizer/Year: Jacobs 1986

Work of Art (MORart) The well-shaped flowers are an orange blend with the reverse slightly more yellow, usually in sprays of three to five. This climbing patio rose can be grown as a pillar rose or as a true climber.

   Parentage: Seedling x Gold Badge
   Hybridizer/Year: Moore 1989

Chapter 4

LANDSCAPING WITH ROSES

'Tigris'

MINIATURE and patio roses can be used in most gardens, formal or informal. They are easy to fit in because they are small, but you can be carried away by catalogues crammed with delicious-looking new varieties, or when visiting a nursery when the roses are in their first flush of flower. You buy more plants than you intended and end up wandering around the garden, plant in hand, trying to find a home for this plant which had seemed so tempting. Shortage of space often means the rose ends up in an unsuitable position in semi-shade or where it cannot thrive in competition with tree or shrub roots. This goes on year after year until the garden becomes a hodgepodge of plants, each in themselves lovely but together a mixture with no cohesiveness and purpose.

It is better for the whole garden to have an overall scheme, taking into account the area of the land, the type of house, how the family lives, and any special horticultural interests.

It is particularly important that small gardens are planned carefully, as the entire area is seen as a whole and the scale and balance or lack of it can be very obvious. Larger gardens may be divided into smaller areas, each with a different theme colour and appropriate plants, depending on the use of each area. These are often referred to as 'garden rooms'. If you have a larger garden, you may want to consider making a part of your garden a 'rose room', where most of the plants are roses or plants which combine well with roses.

It is always easier to start a garden from scratch, where you can find the most suitable places for your favourite plants. But most of us inherit someone else's garden, which is never just as we would have planted it. If you do buy a house with an established garden, it is wise to make very few alterations for 12 months, as there may be all sorts of little treasures in the garden which you unwittingly dig up if you are too impatient.

Whether you are creating a new garden or altering an existing one, the fixed parts, that is paths, patio or terrace, and outbuildings, such as a garden shed or small greenhouse, should be put in place first. Trellises and pergolas can be added for height and to give support for climbing plants. If you are redesigning an existing garden, leave larger trees and shrubs if they can be fitted into your plan, as they give maturity to a garden. Remove only those that are unwanted or in the wrong place.

Small shrubs and conifers can be planted at the back of garden beds to give height, shape and foliage interest. Choose these with care. In a small area no plant should just 'fill a hole'. There are beautiful flowering shrubs such as camellias, hebes or vibernum, shrubs with interesting variegated or coloured foliage and shrubs with scented flowers or foliage.

Miniature and patio roses have a place in every garden. The ideal position is in a well-drained bed which has sun for at least half the day during the summer and with no competition from tree and shrub roots. The soil is friable, containing well-rotted compost and is free of perennial weeds. There should be some shelter from the strongest winds, but not complete shelter. That is the ideal, but rarely are all these conditions attainable. Not only roses will do well with these conditions. Most plants will thrive, except for some shade-loving types.

It is usually suggested that roses be grown in beds on their own. This is often taken to mean beds of hybrid tea and flori-

bunda roses with perhaps a border of miniature roses. If you are growing roses for exhibition this may still be the best way to grow them. However, it is not imperative that you do this. A garden exclusively of roses is not a pretty sight in the winter, with only bare twigs showing for months on end. It may be easier for maintenance if all the roses are in the same area for spraying and dead-heading, but because they are all together insects and disease may be more of a problem than if they are planted among other types of plants.

Over the years, experience has convinced us that roses do well when grown with other plants. Many of the modern roses, particularly miniature, patio and shrub roses, can and should be treated as flowering shrubs. They can add colour and fragrance in front of other plants and can be interplanted with perennials and annuals. We have found that there is less problem with insects and diseases when there are many different types of plants, and the colour and interest in the garden can be extended for 12 months of the year.

Shrub roses should be positioned in the garden wherever you would be planting shrubs. In the last few years many of the world's hybridizers have been producing shrub roses which repeat flower from spring to early winter, are disease free and need little or no maintenance through the year. What more could you ask for in a flowering shrub? These range from modern Rugosa shrubs such as 'Robusta', 'Star Delight' and 'Linda Campbell' to groundcover shrubs such as 'Eyeopener', 'Ferdy' and 'Fairy Moon'. Some flowering shrub roses will have small flowers which could almost be classified as miniature, while others will have flowers as large as floribundas. Many of the David Austin or English roses can also be used in this way. The one

'Drummer Boy'

The miniature climber 'Magic Dragon'.

A miniature rose garden with miniature climbers.

thing they will have in common is an informal flower shape, rather than a hybrid-tea shape flower. Shrub roses grow in different sizes and shapes. There will be tall and slender, tall and wide, medium rounded, short and bushy, and short and wide plants. They are great in the garden and combine well with smaller roses.

We are often asked under what conditions small roses look best in a garden. Although colours do not clash in nature, it is still important that colour is considered before planting. If the garden is mainly pastel pinks and lavenders a miniature rose such as 'Patio Flame' (bright orange) or 'Dorola' (a yellow patio rose) will look out of place. In the same way a soft lavender rose such as 'Sachet' will be lost in a garden bed of yellow day lilies and bronze marigolds.

When they are to be combined with other plants it is advisable to plant 3 or 5 miniature or patio roses together in a group, as a single plant can become lost and overgrown within a season. It is up to you whether to plant 3 or 5 of the same variety, or chose different varieties which tone in well.

Height must also be considered, and the taller plants placed behind the shorter ones. Climbers are very useful on fences and trellises, but they can also be used to give height in a garden where there is no built-in support. Make a tripod of three sturdy stakes at least 2 m long. These should be pushed 30–40 cm into the ground, and attached together in some way at the top. If you are using wooden stakes, drill a hole in the top of each one and fasten the three stakes together with a piece of wire. A climber planted in the centre of this tripod will soon reach the top and the supports will become invisible, leaving only a beautiful column of colour.

Standard or tree roses also give height in the garden. Different nurseries grow their standards at different heights, so if you want them to be the same height in your garden you must check them when purchased. You cannot just bury a taller plant deeper in the ground while planting as it will never thrive. Standards can be underplanted but the miniature roses, perennials or annuals used for this should be low growing. If they are allowed to grow up into the flowering head of the standard, the effect will be lost.

Choose the varieties carefully. A standard rose has been budded onto understock and will grow vigorously. A miniature or patio rose which will grow tall when on its own roots will grow even taller as a standard, and can look very ungainly. There is also the risk that the whole head of the plant could be blown out in a strong wind. Smaller, more compact varieties will be easier to manage and will look better.

Sprawling and arching varieties budded onto a standard will give a weeping effect. For these to be truly appreciated they should be on a reasonably tall stem and have very little or no underplanting. A tall weeping standard can make a spectacular feature in a small island bed in the lawn.

Garden colour schemes

For an all-white garden, try 'Aoraki' for height at the back, then 'Irresistible' and 'Moonlight Lady', graduating down to 'Pacesetter' and 'Gourmet Popcorn' or 'Popcorn', with 'Snow Twinkle', 'Whiteout' and 'Green Ice' in the front. With these roses, Queen Anne's lace, white lavatera

Sprawling varieties can be used as ground cover or to soften walls and fences. Here 'Nozomi' spills over a brick wall.

and white lavender could be interplanted towards the back with white dianthus, violas and alyssum placed nearer the front.

Mauve and lavender gardens can be a little dull if another colour is not introduced. Pink roses are either a yellow pink (salmon or apricot pink) or a blue pink (rose pink or lavender pink). The latter pink combines well with mauves and lavenders. So does white, and yellow may be used with care. Choose one combination, but not all. 'Jeanne Lajoie', the rose pink climber, or 'Aoraki' are ideal for height and in front try lavender roses such as 'Sachet', 'Panache', 'Jennifer', 'Lucky Me', 'Silver', 'Jewel Box', 'Make Believe', 'Sweet Chariot' and 'Winter Magic'. Most dianthus will combine well with these colourings, as will delphiniums, gentians, lavenders, violas, lobelias, forget-me-nots, liatrus, violets, catmint and the lavender alyssum. Some of these roses and other plants will also add fragrance to your garden.

For an all-white garden try the paler shades of 'Whiteout' (above right) and 'Irresistible' (above).

No matter where you live there will always be a good supply of pink roses. But remember that the pink can be either salmon or rose pink, and that the two do not combine well together. Salmon pinks such as 'Little Girl' and 'Angel Pink' (climbers), 'Rexy's Baby', 'Mother's Love', 'Cider Cup', 'Pink Porcelain', 'Sugar 'n' Spice', 'Minnie Pearl' 'Angela Rippon' and many other varieties will look well together. The deep blue delphiniums go well with

'Cider Cup'

pink roses, as do lavateras, pink and blue cornflowers, catmint, white and pink violas, petunias, lobelias, and pink and white alyssum.

Red roses on their own can appear to be sombre and uninteresting. 'Black Jade', 'Patio Prince', 'Dainty Dinah', 'Drummer Boy', 'Mountie', and 'Wee Jock' have different tonings of red, and to add variety there are a number of cultivars with a red and yellow blend which will add interest and glow to the garden. 'San Jose Sunshine', 'Rainbow's End', 'Ring of Fire', 'Chasin' Rainbows', 'Palmetto Sunrise', 'Bay Glow' and 'Pandemonium' all combine well with reds. They can also be used as a transition from a red garden to a yellow garden, leading on to such varieties as 'Rise 'n' Shine', 'Lemon Twist', 'Dorola' and 'My Sunshine'. Day lilies always go well with red and yellow roses, as most are in the red/orange/yellow colours. There are few annual and perennial plants which tone well with only reds, but white violas and alyssum will lighten the area. Or some of the herbs with interesting foliage such as parsley and thyme can be used. If you are introducing the yellow/red colour blends, then the yellow can be enhanced by using marigolds and yellow violas.

'Black Jade' has dark, velvety petals.

Apricot shades, such as those of 'Loving Touch', can be difficult to combine well with other garden plants.

Apricot shades can be difficult to use. 'Loving Touch', 'Party Girl', 'Clarissa', 'Peek a Boo', 'Sweet Dream' and 'Sweet Magic' are some of these. Cream, apricot and pale blue companion plants combine well, such as alyssum, foxgloves, felicia, brachycome and violas.

Where the ground is poor and plants will not readily grow, consider using miniature and patio roses in containers to add colour. Container plants will also give interest and colour to a barren terrace, patio or porch. Hanging baskets will give another dimension, with colour lifted high towards the sky.

Fragrance is important to some gardeners. There are many miniature and patio roses which have some fragrance, and some varieties are very fragrant. It is best to choose fragrant varieties for yourself on a warm still day. Everyone's nose is different, and some can detect a subtle scent which others cannot. But there are some varieties, such as 'Sweet Chariot', 'Sachet', 'Winter Magic' and 'Panache', which even people with a heavy cold could smell!

Planting with roses

It is important to choose perennials and annuals with care if they are to be combined with small-flowered roses. If they have larger flowers than the small rose flowers they can dominate and the roses can be lost in the confusion. There are, however, many small-flowered plants which do well when combined with roses and extend the flowering season of the garden as well as adding to its beauty.

Perennials

Armeria (Thrift): These form short grassy

If you want a heady fragrance in your rose garden, 'Sachet' is a good choice.

Mixed border with small roses.

clumps with pom-pom flowers mainly in white and pink.

Brachycome: These Australian plants form a low mound covered in pink, mauve, lavender, yellow or white small daisies, depending on variety.

Dianthus: There are many varieties available. They range from white through to various shades of pink to red and some have unusual markings. The flowers can be single or double and many are fragrant.

Hemerocallis (Day Lily): These plants deserve to be more widely grown than they are. They come in various shades from maroon through red and orange to yellow, and can be bought as named varieties or as unnamed hybrids. The flax-like leaves are usually 40–60 cm high, and the plants will grow into large clumps which need dividing every few years.

Lamium: There are many different varieties of this ground-cover. Some have variegated or marked leaves, and flowers can be white, pink, yellow or lavender. This plant grows very quickly, and must be watched carefully when close to small roses, as it can almost overwhelm them.

Lavandula (Lavender): These come in white, pink, blue and lavender colours, mostly with green/grey foliage. Both flowers and foliage are fragrant. Cutting back after flowering has finished will give a neater, bushy plant.

Nepeta (Catmint): With its grey-green foliage this looks good all year round, and the spikes of lavender blue flowers are an added bonus. The plants look better if trimmed quite hard every winter. For those gardeners living where they are a problem, it is said that catmint and lavender discourage opossums.

Thymus (Thyme): This low-growing fragrant herb has tiny flowers and some varieties have variegated leaves.

Verbena: There are annual and perennial types of this genus, both of which combine well with small roses. There are many colours and variations of colours, so choose carefully when planting. The lavender/mauve varieties look good with similar coloured roses or white roses.

Violets: Everyone knows and loves violets. They are one of the first harbingers of spring, bringing flowers and fragrance during the bleak winter days when there seems to be nothing else in the garden. They will form a large mat under roses, almost smothering the smaller plants if allowed to grow rampant. It is best to control the growth every year or at the least every second year by digging up and dividing the plants. The leftover divisions can be easily potted up into spare containers and given away and are always an acceptable gift. Unfortunately violets can be a refuge for spider mite, and must be sprayed regularly when spraying the roses.

Annuals

Alyssum: This annual forms a carpet of tiny flowers which self-seed every year and

Miniature and patio roses combine well to create an interesting border.

can become so prolific that it will smother annual weeds and even small roses if allowed to grow without check. The most common variety has white flowers, but it also comes in pink, apricot and lavender shades. It combines well with even the smallest roses.

Lobelia: A low-growing plant which comes in blue, blue/white, and pink colourings. Plants are either short and bushy or trailing, and will self-seed if left in the ground until the autumn. There are also perennial lobelia in various colours. The form and tall spiky shape of these plants adds some variety in the rose garden.

Marigolds: These come in many colours, from cream to bright sulphur yellow through to bronze. Do not plant near rose pink shades of roses. Marigolds are reputed to have a deterrent effect against nematodes or eel worms.

Myosotis (Forget-Me-Not): This plant, with tiny white, blue or pink flowers, grows to about 25 cm and can become invasive if all the seedlings are allowed to grow every year. With judicious culling of unwanted plants, it can blend well with roses, particularly in a cottage garden.

Parsley: This annual herb with its curly bright green foliage looks good against brighter colours in the flower garden. Do not use in cooking if the plants around it have been sprayed.

Violas and Pansies: Although the flowers of these are usually as big or slightly bigger than those of miniature roses, the plants are normally shorter and they combine well. Violas and pansies will flower through to late autumn and even winter in temperate climates, giving some colour when the roses have finished. These will self-seed, but will not necessarily come true to colour year after year. The small *Viola tricolor,* sometimes known as Heartsease or Johnny Jump-Up, with its cheeky tiny flowers in combinations of yellow and blue will quickly become a nuisance if allowed to seed too freely. But it is still a worthwhile plant to add to the cottage garden.

Chapter 5

ROSES IN CONTAINERS

'Warm Welcome'

MINIATURE and patio roses grow well in pots and containers. In fact it is sometimes the only way space can be found for an extra plant or a particularly choice variety. The term 'patio rose' does not necessarily mean that all varieties grouped under this name will look good growing in a container on a patio or terrace; as with miniature roses, the correct selection of variety for the particular growing situation is important. Not only should the eventual height of the plant be taken into consideration, but the shape of the bush, habit of growth, type of flower and colour should all be borne in mind before a decision is made. Much can depend on the overall effect you want.

Types of containers

Clay or plastic? Wood or concrete? Both plastic and terracotta will give equal suc-cess. The choice is yours. Consideration must be given to your overall garden design, as some plastic pots are not as aesthetically pleasing as terracotta or pottery and come in colours which do not blend in with the landscape. Wooden tubs and barrels are also suitable, but make sure they have been made from untreated timber. A terracotta or clay pot which is not sealed or glazed absorbs moisture from the mix and the plant will therefore dry out more quickly than it would in a plastic container.

Size is more important than the type of pot. Small pots of 2 litres or less can be used for small miniature roses such as 'Stacey Sue' or 'Whiteout' for a season or two, but if you want your miniature or patio roses to grow to a size comparable with those grown in the open ground you will need a pot at least 5 litres or larger. A

A basket of 'Nozomi'.

utilitarian container may be placed inside a more decorative pot, and several plastic pots may be placed inside a trough. If you do this, the spaces between the pots can be filled with sawdust or sphagnum moss which will help to retain moisture as well as hide the pots.

Regardless of size, the best containers for roses will be those with a greater depth than width. The smaller the container, the more quickly the mix will dry out, and therefore the more often it will have to be watered; the larger the container the longer it can be left between waterings. Another plus is that large pots do not blow over so easily in windy conditions.

Miniature and patio roses can also be grown in hanging baskets. Wire baskets lined with coconut fibre or sphagnum moss look more natural than those lined with plastic, but do lose more moisture from transpiration. Plastic hanging baskets are also available and work well. Water-absorbent crystal gel is almost a necessity for hanging baskets as they dry out very quickly and are difficult to water.

Suitable sites

One of the benefits of having plants in containers is that they can be used where plants would not otherwise grow. Obvious places are patios and terraces, but don't overlook stony areas of the garden or close to trees and hedges where root competition may be too great for plants in the ground. Containers are also useful because they are so easily moved. They can be used to give instant colour where needed, and when necessary can be replaced with ease.

All roses do better when they are given the correct amount of light, sun and shelter. You can place pots in full sun or dappled

Pot-grown miniature roses are ideal for patios and terraces.

'Angelita' growing in a container.

shade. During the winter, when the plants are dormant and not at their best, they can be placed somewhere out of sight, only to be brought back into view when they are in full leaf and bud again in the spring.

Miniature and patio roses are not indoor plants. They do not do well in conservatories or living rooms where the surrounding air is too dry and there is not enough light. If you want to enjoy your roses inside, bring the container in when the rose is in bud, but as soon as the flowers are finished cut the dead heads off, fertilize and put outside until the next flush of flowers appears.

General care and maintenance

Looking after miniature and patio roses in containers is rather like looking after a baby — you must provide everything that is needed for their health and well-being. Unlike a plant growing in the ground, a plant in a container can absorb moisture from only a small area, and it cannot take advantage of any residual fertilizer or trace elements left in the soil, as these leach through very quickly in containers. You must give your potted roses these things regularly.

A commercial potting mix is the best planting medium for container roses. Garden soil cakes and dries like concrete, and contains weed seeds and other nasties. Potting mix is sterile, free draining, and most contain some form of slow-release fertilizer, which will last the first few months. Not all potting mixes are created equal. Check carefully. A peat-based potting mix can shrink away from the sides of the pot when dry, making it difficult to wet thoroughly again. A crushed bark-based potting mix does not shrink when dry, and is very free draining. When planting, use some form of water-absorbent crystal gel for moisture retention.

Transplant your chosen rose carefully, making sure that it is not buried any deeper than it was planted originally. It is important at this stage to give the plant a good deep water, as sometimes the potting mix is dry and can be difficult to saturate. If you are planting a small miniature rose into a large container, planting annuals around the edge of the pot at the same time will give a better display for the first season.

More pot plants have died from watering problems than any other cause. As far as miniature and patio roses are concerned, water is the secret of success. During the warmer weather when the plants are growing strongly, small pots need to be watered nearly every day and plants in very large pots need water every second or third day. Different types of potting mixes vary in texture and drainage capacity so check the plants regularly, as this watering regime may not be suitable for your particular conditions. More water may be needed if the mix is very light and free draining, or the plants may become too soggy in a heavy mix. Watch containers with saucers. If water collects and remains in the saucer for too long, the mix in the bottom of the container is sure to become too wet and the plant roots may rot. If a water-absorbent crystal gel has been added to the mix when planting this does not mean that you don't have to water, but it is a good back-up which can save a plant from dehydration on the days when we all forget to water and should have!

Because the water drains out through the holes in the base, taking with it nutrients from the potting mix, plants in pots need to be fertilized regularly. Any general purpose fertilizer may be used. Small pots can be top dressed with ½ to 1 teaspoonful of fertilizer, and larger pots would get a little more. This should be applied in the early spring as growth starts, and again whenever the plants are trimmed after flowering. As well, a liquid fertilizer in a weak solution can be added every time spray is applied. If you prefer, a slow-release fertilizer can be used, but check on the label, as some last for three months, six months or nine months. They do not necessarily last

for a full growing season.

Miniature and patio roses grown in containers give the best results when trimmed back regularly. As soon as the flowers have faded, the stems should be cut back a little harder than if the plants were grown in the garden. This encourages basal breaks and gives bushier plants with good foliage and quick repeat flowering. Applying a little fertilizer around the plant at this time encourages new growth more quickly. It is an inbred characteristic of many miniature roses that strong basal shoots grow up above the natural height of the plant. These shoots often have candelabra-type heads. They can be treated in two ways. Either pinch out the end of the strong shoot when it is still immature and has not reached the natural plant height, or leave it to flower (staking with a bamboo cane if necessary) and when all the flowers have finished cut back to the lowest side shoot, leaving only one or two leaves on the side shoot.

Plants in containers need the same attention to pests and diseases as those in the garden. If you have taken a plant indoors to flower, take it outside again before spraying. A strong spray of water with the hose may solve an insect problem.

It is sometimes said that miniature roses should be taken out of their pots every year and repotted. Why? How often do you replant the roses in your garden? If you don't replant garden roses, why should you replant pot roses? Every year in the winter clean the rubbish and any weeds from the top of the container and top up with fresh potting mix. If a plant is not performing as well as it should, tip it out of the pot, cut about 5 cm of potting mix and roots from the base with a sharp knife, replace this with fresh potting mix in the bottom of the container and firm the plant back into position. This gives the plant a new lease on life and new roots will soon grow and seek out the fresh potting mix. Never remove all

Tall slender roses like 'Pink Petticoat' give height in large containers.

the potting mix from around the roots unless there are obvious signs of fungal disease. With regular watering and feeding in a container of adequate size any miniature or patio rose should do well indefinitely.

If you are going away on holiday during the summer, care of containers depends on how long you will be away. If it is only for a few days, give the plants a thorough water, place in semi-shade and they should look fine when you get home. If you will be away for longer, say two weeks, and cannot persuade a reliable neighbour to water your plants regularly, the safest way is to dig a trench in the garden where there is semi-shade and put all your pots into the trench. Cover the pots up to the rims with compost, soil or sawdust and water thoroughly just before leaving. Be careful when uplifting the plants when you get home as roots may have grown through the drainage hole to seek more moisture.

If by some mischance your container

plant does get dry and the leaves turn brown and shrivel, it does not necessarily mean that your plant is dead. If the stems are still green, cut the growth back quite hard and give it a good soaking. Plunge the pot into a container of water if possible. Within a few days the plant should begin to make new growth.

If the roses have been trimmed regularly through the growing season there should be very little to do in the way of winter pruning. When you do the winter weeding and clean up, cut back any dead stems and trim out thin spindly growth, particularly from the centre of the plant. This may be all that is necessary, as the top growth will be neat and tidy from regular dead-heading. If the plant has grown taller than you wish, cut back healthy stems by up to half their height.

Roses suitable for container growing

As with garden roses, varieties for containers should be chosen with care. Almost any miniature or patio rose will grow in a pot, but some will look better than others. Decide what effect you want. A neat, rounded, bushy plant covered in flowers is what most people consider the ideal container plant. This can be achieved with many varieties, including 'Whiteout,' Jewel Box', 'Si', 'Noelle Marie' or 'Kaikoura.' Remember to match container size to variety. Use small pots for 'Si' and other small varieties, and larger pots for taller varieties like 'Kaikoura.' Some of the more informal sprawling varieties such as 'The Fairy', 'Green Ice', 'Kapiti', 'Flower Carpet' and 'Sweet Chariot' can look marvellous in the right container in the right spot. Tall slender plants such as 'Clarissa', 'Pink Petticoat', or even 'Little Girl' can be used to give height in a large container, with short miniature roses or annuals such as alyssum, lobelia or pansies planted to fill the pot and soften the edge.

Container plants are usually grown for

A hanging basket of 'Green Ice'.

colour. They may be used to pick up or accentuate some feature of the house or garden or to lighten a dull area. The more informal open flowers and varieties with larger semi-double flowers will give more colour in containers than the hybrid-tea type flowers, which have more individual beauty and are better for picking.

The roses you grow in containers should be chosen with even more care than those in your garden. While roses which take longer to repeat flower can be disguised in the garden situation by nearby plantings of perennials and annuals, in a container a rose which is flowerless for weeks or sometimes even months on end can be a disappointment.

For a formal garden, standard or tree roses grown in containers fit in very well. The container will have to be reasonably large, as a mature standard miniature or patio rose can become top heavy in a small container and will blow over in wind.

Varieties such as 'Angelita', 'Bay Glow' and 'Chasin' Rainbows' will give a small rounded head, while others like 'Pink Bells', 'The Fairy', 'Nozomi' and 'Sea Foam' will spread and arch, giving a weeping or semi-weeping effect.

Some experimentation will show you the best varieties to use in hanging baskets. It may depend on the effect you wish to create. 'Green Ice', 'The Fairy' and 'Kapiti' will arch gracefully over the sides of the basket. But I have also seen baskets planted with 'Stacey Sue', with deep blue lobelia trailing around the edges. 'High Spirits' was also spectacular, with white alyssum planted through the wire basket to create a white base.

Growing plants in containers can be very rewarding. Growing roses in containers can be specially rewarding. Their care is very similar to that required by garden roses. There are no special formulas, no secret recipes, just common sense and a sensitivity to the plants and their requirements.

Chapter 6

ROSES IN THE HOME

A rose potpourri.

SMALL roses are not only a joy in the garden; they also give endless satisfaction and pleasure when picked. They can be used for many types of arrangements, as well as small posies, which are always well received as gifts. Building a collection of small containers to arrange miniature and patio roses in can be quite a challenge. Think laterally. There are many small vases and bowls which can be used, but for those very miniature roses think of sea-shells, lipstick holders, thimbles, ornamental salt shakers, and even dolls' tea-sets. You are only limited by your imagination.

All roses last better when picked several hours after a deep watering. Take a container with 3–5 cm of warm water with you to the garden, and as soon as the roses are picked place them in this. Once back inside, add cold water almost to the top of

the stem. Be careful that the blooms are not under the water. Leave for several hours or preferably overnight before using in an arrangement. The blooms are now conditioned and should last nearly a week.

A small vase with just a few perfect blooms in it looks great on a table or window ledge, but with a little more effort the arrangement can be made more interesting. Some sprigs of gypsophila, maidenhair fern or Queen Anne's lace add another dimension. Other flowers can be included, too, but make sure that they are not larger than the rose blooms as they can dominate and take away the interest from the roses. Small airy flowers such as dianthus, cornflower, verbena, brachycome and the small asters combine well with roses. If foliage is required, light lacy types such as maidenhair or asparagus fern are suitable and bronze fennel looks great.

Small posies and tussie-mussies can be constructed in the same way. By walking around the garden and selecting roses and other flowers and foliage an interesting little posy can be constructed in no time. Arrange these flowers in your hand as you go, and when finished hold together with a rubber band. A little florist's paper and ribbon bow finish it off, and you have a very welcome gift for a hospital patient or friend.

Small *unsprayed* rose buds can be used in ice cubes for a festive occasion. Fill the ice cube tray about one-third and freeze. Then add a rose bud to each cube, fill with water and freeze again. Ice cubes done in this way can be used in individual drinks or floating in a large punch bowl.

No matter how long roses bloom and how much they are appreciated during the warmer months, there is always the desire to enjoy them year-round. This can be done by harvesting flowers and even petals when they are in full flush.

All roses, including miniature and patio roses, can be dried. The easiest method is to gather a bunch of half-open blooms, tie the bunch with twine and hang it upside down from the ceiling of a dry, dark room. The garage or garden shed will be ideal for this purpose. It is important to pick the flowers when they are at their driest, which is usually about mid-day or soon after. Roses treated in this way should be left hanging upside down until completely dry.

Rose buds can also be preserved in silica gel. With this method, the stem is usually cut off and only the flower head is dried. Once again it is important that the blooms are completely dry before adding the silica gel. Cover the bottom third of a suitable container with silica gel, then carefully place the flowers on it. The flowers must

'Heart 'n' Soul' makes a beautiful table arrangement.

There are 100 blooms and buds in this miniature rose bouquet.

be completely covered with the gel, and the easiest way is to use a teaspoon, as it is most important that the small crystals go between the petals. The container can then be covered and left in a cool dark place so that the roses dry gradually.

If the container is plastic or glass it can be left uncovered and processed in a microwave oven for one or two minutes. The time will vary depending on the power of the oven and the number of flowers you are doing at one time. It is important to have a glass of water in the microwave to prevent plant material of any sort from burning once the moisture content has gone. Experiment with a few roses at first until you find out what suits your conditions best. Have a look at the roses after the suggested processing time. Gently brush the crystals away from the petals with a camel hair brush or something similar, making sure that the flower is completely dry. If it is not quite ready, put back into the microwave for a few seconds more. (I believe that it is possible to use kitty litter in place of silica gel, but I have not tried it.)

If the dried buds are to be used in a flower arrangement, put a piece of florist's wire through the calyx and twist the ends together. The wire can be covered with a green florist's tape to make it look more like stems if you wish. Store dried flowers in an airtight container with a small amount of silica gel. The dried buds can also add colour and interesting texture to potpourri and for this the smaller miniatures are ideal.

Roses often change colour when dried. Lighter coloured varieties seem to retain their original colour better than darker ones; reds often look purple or black when dried. Experiment with various varieties. It is important to label varieties before drying, as they can sometimes be hard to identify afterwards.

Rose petals can easily be dried for use in potpourri. Gather dry petals from fully opened flowers, preferably the highly scented ones, and place in a shallow box in a warm place. Stir gently with your hands several times a day until the petals are fully dried and crispy to the touch. Do not keep adding more petals over several days, as the nearly dry ones will absorb moisture from the fresh petals. Other potpourri ingredients can be dried in the same way. If you are in a hurry, petals can be dried between paper towels in a microwave; rosemary, lavender, geranium and mint leaves take about one minute, depending on the number of leaves.

Some recipes using roses

These recipes will help you to enjoy the fruits of your rose garden even in the bleak winter. It is important that any rose petals used for cosmetics or for eating must be taken from roses which have not been sprayed.

Old Fashioned Rose Potpourri

2 cups dry rose petals
½ cup dry rose geranium leaves
½ cup dry lavender flowers
½ cup dry carnation petals
2 tablespoons sweet marjoram
2 tablespoons dry crumbled orange peel
1 tablespoon whole cloves
1 tablespoon orris root
A few drops rose oil
½ cup dried miniature rose buds

Combine all ingredients and let age for four weeks.

Rosewater

2 parts petals to 1 part hot water

Blend well in blender, simmer 15 minutes, strain. Repeat until you get the desired strength, using the rosewater produced and adding more petals. Always use glass, enamel or stainless steel equipment.

Rosewater can be used in many ways. It

Use a variety of your favourite rose petals to create your own rose potpourri.

is wonderful for the skin as an aid to wrinkles and dryness, puffiness, eczema or large pores. Always keep in the refrigerator.

Rosewater Hand Softener
3 teaspoons cornflour
150 ml rosewater
1 teaspoon lemon juice
2 tablespoons glycerine

Mix cornflour with rosewater and heat slightly. Add glycerine and lemon juice and heat until it has started to thicken, stirring all the time. Keep in the refrigerator.

Muscle Soothing Bath
½ cup bay leaves
1 cup rosewater
1 cup water

Simmer 1 cup water and bay leaves for 5 minutes. Steep for 10 minutes. Add rosewater. Strain directly into bath. The leaves of the bay plant have always been a remedy for tired muscles.

Sleep Pillow
6 cups dry rose petals
1–2 cups dry mint leaves
2½ tablespoons crushed cloves
small amount of dried sweet basil
 (optional)

Mix well together and place in small square pillow made of close-weave cotton. The pillow can be placed inside the pillowcase with your ordinary pillow, or used on top. This will help you sleep and is small enough to take with you when travelling.

Chapter 7

ROSES UNDER COVER

'Radiant'

MOST miniature and patio roses grow well under cover and this adds another facet to your pleasure, as it increases the length of the flowering season and gives you somewhere to work and enjoy your roses in cold or wet weather. There is an increasing interest in growing miniature and patio roses as cut flowers for the home or for the commercial market; in most cases this means growing the plants under some type of cover. The cover can be some high-tech glasshouse with all the bells and whistles, or it can be a small plastic or shadecloth-covered homemade structure which will give some protection from the elements. Often it is something in between.

The main reason for growing the plants under cover is to give some control over the growing conditions and to protect the plants from weather extremes. Roses grown under cover in unheated houses will flower several weeks earlier in the spring and continue to flower later in the autumn, but will not flower through the winter, as flowering depends not only on shelter and warmth, but also on day length. If you are constructing your own greenhouse, make sure that there is plenty of ventilation and air circulation, otherwise during the heat of the summer the roses can literally cook if the temperature cannot be kept down. The ideal is to have the inside temperature no higher than the outside during the summer, and up to 10 degrees warmer than the outside temperature during the spring and autumn. Shadecloth can help keep temperatures down in the summer, but must be taken off during autumn, winter and spring or it will suppress light to such an extent that there will be fewer flowers and the plants will become very drawn.

If you want to extend your growing season even more you could try growing under lights. In its simplest form this means using a double fluorescent light fitting suspended low over a row of plants in pots. Use reflectors, aluminium foil or white board to concentrate the light on the plants. Keep the lights on for about 16 hours a day. You may also need some way to keep your growing chamber warmer on cold, frosty nights. In this way you can have miniature roses in flower over winter.

Roses under cover can be planted directly into the ground or in containers. We have also seen miniature roses grown very successfully using hydroponics, but this requires specialised equipment and growing conditions.

If you are growing the plants in the ground, consider raising the beds by up to 25 cm. This ensures that the drainage is good, and also makes it easier to pick the blooms. The ground must be well prepared. Spray first with weedkiller, then after the recommended waiting period dig or rotary hoe the ground thoroughly. Incorporate compost, well-rotted sawdust, old animal manure or any other available material which will add humus to the soil and help with drainage and water-holding capacity. Keep this prepared ground watered well and wait several weeks for weeds to germinate. Fork out any perennial weeds which appear and hoe out the small annual weeds. Time taken at this stage will save time, effort and money later.

Miniature and patio roses grown for cutting can be planted closer together than the plants grown in the garden. But it can depend on the variety. 'Pacesetter', being tall and upright, can be grown 15–20 cm apart, while you should allow at least 30 cm for plants of 'Minnie Pearl', which grow more bushy and spreading. Bushes planted close together become self-supporting and

should need no staking. Do not make the rows of plants too wide, as picking becomes difficult and the blooms in the centre are often left because they cannot be reached.

If you prefer to grow the plants in containers, make sure that the containers are large enough. A 20-litre pot is the smallest size in which to grow a miniature rose well for cut flower production, and an even larger pot would be better for the average patio rose. Pots can be set on benches 25–30 cm high, making the plants easily accessible without too much bending or stooping. Planting mixes should be the same as for any rose grown in a container.

Plant management is most important when growing under cover. As always with roses, watering is the first and main essential. For plants grown in the ground, some type of automatic or semi-automatic system such as sprinklers on stakes works well. Ideally these should be in place before the roses are planted and can be on a timer or turned on and off as required. As the plants grow, check to make sure that the water is still being spread evenly on the ground around the roots of the plants. The foliage can sometimes divert the water and leave dry patches which are only noticed when the foliage starts to burn and crisp up. 'Leaky' hoses or soak hoses left in place along the rows will also work well. When the chosen watering system is in place, turn on for at least two hours and every 15 minutes check the depth the water has reached. You then know how long to leave the hose turned on for adequate watering. Remember that deep watering as required is better than a frequent shallow sprinkle.

Watering roses in containers is easy with modern technology. There are a number of different types of drippers on the market, most of them are attached to small diameter laterals coming off the main pipe and inserted one to a container. These drippers can also be used for plants in the ground, but two per plant may be required as the water will disperse further. Once again it is important when first installed to check the amount of water being given to each plant. Don't take the salesman's word — check for yourself. The pressure you have may be quite different from one used for the manufacturer's trials.

Miniature and patio roses grow under cover much as they do outside, but they will probably grow larger, and with longer stems. With the stronger growth and constant picking, more fertilizer will be needed for these plants than for plants grown outside. Some fertilizers leach through the soil in a few weeks. Other slow-release fertilizers will last several months. Check the active life of your fertilizer and apply whenever required while the plants are producing blooms.

Because the plants are growing quite close together, disease prevention and control is important, otherwise problems can go through the greenhouse like wildfire. Ventilation is most important during the summer, as hot humid conditions encourage fungal diseases such as powdery mildew, rust, black spot and downy mildew. Good hygiene is essential. Don't leave dead flowers and leaves on the ground or on paths between roses. Pick off dead or dying flowers to prevent botrytis, particularly in the autumn. Unless carefully controlled, greenfly can be a problem on the soft, lush growth. Mites love the hot dry conditions of high summer. Read again the chapter on insect and disease controls and spray regularly.

If you are interested in selling cut flowers, do some market research before deciding on varieties to plant. This can be as simple as talking to your local florist or visiting the flower auction in your area. Several things are important. Find out if there is an interest in miniature and patio roses, who wants

Bouquet of 'Deep Velvet' and white carnations.

them and when. If there is a demand, make sure that you can provide the flowers when they are needed. You may have to experiment with cutting back plants so that they will flower when florists need them most. It is disappointing to have many bunches of lovely blooms ready two weeks before St Valentine's Day when no-one wants them, and nothing to pick two weeks later when the price is up and the demand is there. The next question to ask is what colours are the most popular. Fashion often dictates what colours are in demand. The small roses are very popular for wedding work and white and cream flowers are always suitable for this. Experiment with only one or two plants of deep colours until you are certain that they are right for your particular market.

Some varieties will perform differently under cover; some will be much paler, and a few will become more intense. Experiment with a few plants of each variety at the beginning until you know how they will perform in your conditions.

Roses for picking must have a good bud shape and a suitable number of petals so that they open slowly when picked. They must come on straight stems which are of good length in proportion to the size of the bloom. Some markets require a single bloom per stem, and some prefer many flowers per stem. If the latter, the flowers should ideally all open at about the same time so that you are not wasting a lot of green buds which will not open.

Well-conditioned cut flowers will last longer. Pick flowers into 3–5 cm of pleasantly warm water and as soon as you have finished picking fill the container with cold water almost up to the top of the stem. Be careful that the blooms are not under water. Leave the container of flowers in a dry cool place overnight. They are now conditioned and should last for a week.

The following is a list of some suggested varieties grouped by colour:

White/Cream	Irresistible, Moonlight Lady, Pacesetter, Luis Desamero
Pale Pink	Minnie Pearl, Pink Porcelain, Sugar 'n Spice
Red	Patio Prince, Deep Velvet, Black Jade
Yellow	Dorola, Clarissa, Little Nugget
Orange	Patio Flame, Radiant
Bi-Colour	Pink Petticoat, Little Jackie
Apricot	Jean Kenneally, Loving Touch, Party Girl
Lavender	Silver, Winter Magic, Winsome

Chapter 8

SHARING YOUR ROSES

A bouquet of dried roses.

WHENEVER we do something well we love to share it with others. It may be singing, painting, country dancing or woodwork. It may be growing miniature and patio roses. We have a friend in Dallas, Texas, who each year cuts thousands of blooms from his miniature roses. He gives them by the hundred to people in hospital or sick at home; for decoration in the church; for weddings and funerals; to the girls who serve in the restaurant where he has breakfast. He says he has pleasure in growing them but greater pleasure when he sees the joy on the faces of those to whom he has given roses.

You can also share by showing them. Rose shows can vary from your local garden club to a National Rose Show and will differ from country to country. All rose shows have some things in common. The judges will be looking for good, clean exhibits. This means that the bloom and leaves will be fresh and free from damage from disease, insects and the weather. The bloom must also be at the right stage, usually the stage which makes the flower most attractive; not too tight but not too far open, unless this is what is required. Remember that a rose has leaves and these are part of the exhibit and must be shown on a stem of suitable length. In America, where judging is by variety, the judge will be looking for the best 'Black Jade', 'Jean Kenneally' or 'Irresistible'; in England it is often a vase or bowl of three, five or more blooms which are required, while in New Zealand judges are looking for the best exhibition bloom or the best stem of miniature roses.

All this may seem a little confusing. If you are interested in showing your roses, go to

A charming bouquet of 'Little Woman'.

Basket of 'Jean Kenneally' at the American Rose Show.

1520 miniature roses picked for distribution to various charities.

your local rose shows and look at the exhibits. Ask questions. A true enthusiast likes nothing better than to talk roses. Join your local garden club or rose society.

One of the good things about showing miniature roses is that they are easily transported. Because of their size, it is easy to put a few chosen blooms in a box and fly off several hundred kilometres to some rose show. Perhaps the ultimate in long distant showing is done by Dr Thomas Cairns of California, who has regularly taken miniature roses to England where he competes very successfully. If you have any thought about taking roses across an international border, check beforehand to find out whether this is allowed and for any restrictions which may be associated with this.

Even if you have no interest in showing your roses, go to the local rose show. This is an excellent way to see some of the newer roses and check on those which grow well in your area. One word of warning, though. Sometimes the best variety in the show is not the best variety for a garden. Ask some questions before you rush off and order that new miniature rose.

Chapter 9

CARING FOR YOUR ROSES

'Sugar'n'Spice'

Climate

ALL roses, whatever their type, have the same basic physical requirements of soil and climate, but some species have adapted better to extremes of cold or inadequate water than others. It is interesting that no wild roses were found in the Southern Hemisphere; they belong in the temperate and cooler areas across Europe, Asia and North America. They certainly seem to grow better in areas which have a definite cold season and may need the cold for the seed to germinate. Perhaps they were unable to adapt naturally to the heat and humidity of the tropics which formed a climatic barrier between north and south.

It has frequently been said that the best roses in the world grow in New Zealand. If this is true, it is because of the climatic conditions. Nowhere is far from the sea and because of this there are no great extremes of temperature as in continental Europe, Asia and North America. The summers are warm and in some areas, pleasantly hot. Although New Zealanders often complain of the cold and frosts that are common in many parts of the country, the winters are relatively mild with significant regular snowfalls at higher altitudes only. Nowhere do we have the bitter, harsh winters of northern Europe and North America; nor do we have the lack of water and near desert conditions found in many other places. Over much of the country rainfall is adequate, although extra water may have to be given to roses in the hottest months of the summer.

There are other places in other countries

In harsh climates most modern roses need to be protected from the worst of the cold. Here each rose bush is covered by a polystyrene cone.

with similar climatic conditions. On the Pacific coast of North America in parts of Oregon, Washington and across into British Columbia we found roses as we expect to see them in New Zealand. The same was true in Ireland and southern England, and in parts of Australia, and we are sure there are other places we have yet to visit.

Rose growers have pushed back the boundaries of where roses can be grown sucessfully. Sometimes it needs little more than a gentle nudge. Roses grow well in places like Georgia or Florida in the United States, but the greater heat of summer makes them grow more quickly and the flowers do not have a chance to develop to

the size of those which experience cooler summers. The humidity can also increase the problem of fungal diseases.

Elsewhere, pushing back the boundaries requires a gigantic heave. It is hard for those living in a relatively mild climate to appreciate the cold of a northern winter in Europe or North America. You must live through days of sub-zero temperatures to know what cold really is. And yet roses are grown under these conditions. Some of the species roses and their near offspring require very little protection, but most modern roses must be protected from the worst of the cold and especially the biting winds which lower temperatures even further.

This is also true of miniature and patio roses. Although miniature roses are generally more hardy than the larger roses, and especially the hybrid teas, in very cold areas they do need some winter protection. Perhaps surprisingly, in some situations all they will require is a blanket of snow, or a wall or fence to break the wind. A covering of leaves or soil over the base of the plant, leaving only the longer tips exposed, may also suffice in all but the coldest places. With extreme cold, elaborate covers may be used to protect the large roses and similar methods may be necessary if miniature roses are to be successfully grown outside over the winter. Of course the simplest way to grow these small roses under these conditions is in containers, which can be moved to sheltered areas of the garden or the garage or basement for the winter.

At the other extreme, roses are also grown in arid areas such as parts of California or Nevada. Here they can grow well provided sufficient water is available. Once again the heat can make the flowers develop quickly so that their size is reduced, but the dry air can discourage the pests and diseases which normally attack roses.

Any description of the care and cultivation of roses cannot ignore these extremes but, in general, unless mention is made of them, we will be considering more moderate conditions.

General care

Contrary to popular belief, roses do not require constant care. Even the small roses are much more hardy than you may think. There are, however, a few things to watch for.

Spraying for pests and diseases often comes to mind when considering rose care, but the amount of spraying you do depends upon the roses you grow, the time that you have and what you are prepared to put up with. (Spraying is dealt with in detail in Chapter 11, Pests and Diseases.)

More important than spraying is watering. Roses do not like to become too dry. If the days are hot and dry and there has been little rain the roses will probably need water. Remember that a good soaking once a week is better than a frequent light sprinkle. Lack of water will not kill established roses but it will limit their growth, causing stunted bushes. Water is particularly important for newly planted roses, as without it the new roots will not be encouraged to grow and the bush will die or at best remain small. I well remember two sisters who bought identical roses and each took one home to plant in their own gardens. A year later they were back again and commented on the progress of the roses they had bought. One rose bush had grown and flourished and was a strong, healthy bush; the other was small, much the same size as it had been when purchased. After some discussion it became clear that the difference was watering — one sister did, the other didn't.

Roses, like all growing things need feeding, and to do well they need a good balanced diet. When you buy fertilizer you will often see numbers such as 8-4-10. This is the NPK ratio, the percentage of nitrogen (N), phosphorus (P), and potassium (K), the primary nutrients for all plant growth, in the fertilizer. While all three are essential, each is particularly responsible for different aspects of growth: nitrogen encourages growth in general and is vital for those wonderful green leaves; phosphorus promotes good roots, and potassium hardens the stems and adds to the flower colour.

Also needed are the trace elements, so called because they are only required in very small amounts. They are essential to plant growth, too, and of these, iron and magnesium are probably the most important for roses. The other trace elements, such as manganese or boron, are generally found in adequate quantities in our soil.

Roses should be fed in the early spring as the soil warms up, and again after the first flush of bloom finishes. Scatter the fertilizer around your bushes, don't just drop it in a heap close to the centre. Smaller amounts should be given to smaller roses, and nothing to newly planted roses. If you are looking for a good display in autumn, a little feeding in late summer will help.

What fertilizer should be used? For most purposes a general fertilizer is adequate, with an NPK ratio of about 8-4-10 being the closest to ideal for roses. You might like to add a little extra nitrogen in the early summer to encourage leaf growth. In the early autumn, less nitrogen is required but a little extra potash (potassium) will help to harden the growth before the arrival of winter.

Your roses will sometimes indicate that a change to their diet is needed. This shows up particularly in the colour of the leaves. If the leaves are not a healthy deep green perhaps your roses are not getting enough nitrogen. If it is some time since they were last fed, perhaps the nutrient has been completely used or leached from the soil.

The leaves may show a definite yellow coloration or streaking. This may be caused by a nutrient deficiency. When the plants are receiving adequate general fertilizer, the most common deficiencies are caused by shortages of magnesium or iron. Use a mixture of one teaspoon (about 5 grams) of magnesium sulphate (Epsom salts) and a pinch of iron chelate to 5 litres of water. (You can use small quantities of mixed trace elements if you have no source of the separate ingredients.) When the soil is wet, water this mixture over the plant. (Some of the material may be absorbed through the leaves.) This solution will act more quickly than dry material sprinkled on the ground. If you are concerned about the general health of your plants, a little extra magnesium and a touch of iron can do them all good.

Don't confuse deficiencies with discol-

Miniature standard or tree roses in California watered by flood irrigation due to the near desert conditions.

oration due to natural ageing or disease. As the season advances, it is quite natural for some of the older leaves low on the bush to begin to turn yellow and eventually drop off. It is only when the new growth high on the bush begins to turn yellow that you have a problem.

Plants can only use the elements in the soil when they are available and they are only available when they are in a form that can be dissolved in water. Dry fertilizer should never be applied to dry soil. Perhaps the most important 'fertilizer' we can give roses is water, because although roses can be fed, without water they may starve.

Do pick your roses. Modern miniature and patio roses repeat flower but they will do so more quickly if the flowers are cut for use in a vase or after they have dropped when left to wither on the bush. Cutting encourages new growth and this brings more flowers.

Don't get too bogged down in a routine of watering, feeding, spraying and pruning — take the time to enjoy your roses. If you can't do this, why grow them?

Chapter 10

PLANTING

'White Pet'

Where?

ROSES will tolerate a variety of soil types. While a good silty loam is ideal, they can be successfully grown in soils ranging from sand to heavy clay. If your soil is very sandy, you may wish to add compost or peat to improve its water-holding capacity. If it is very heavy, sand or compost will help to open it up.

One thing roses will not tolerate is wet feet. If the area where you plan to grow your roses is not well drained this should be attended to before the roses are planted. You may need to provide drainage of some type, or you may decide to raise the rose beds above the level of their surroundings.

Even in the hottest places roses can be grown in full sun provided they receive sufficient water. Strong sunlight can affect the colour of some. Yellows and pinks may fade to creams and whites, while some reds will burn. These varieties will do better with some shade, particularly from the early afternoon sun. Too much shade will encourage growth at the expense of flowers and it is usually suggested that at least half a day's sun is ideal.

Some varieties need shade to bring out their unusual colouring. When grown in full sun the open flower of 'Green Ice' is a creamy white. In partial shade the flowers will be a soft pale green. Other varieties need sunlight. This is especially true of those combining reds and yellows. 'Rainbow's End' is a delightful combination of red on yellow when growing in sufficient sunlight. Grown in the shade it may become just a yellow rose.

If possible, dig over your new rose bed a month or two before the roses are to be

'Sweet Chariot'

planted. Open it up to the sun and air. At this time any compost or natural fertilizer that you have access to can be included, provided it will have time to be incorporated fully into the soil before the roses are planted.

What?

When selecting roses for your garden, care should be taken to choose the right type of rose for the purpose and place for which it is intended.

If you are ordering new roses by mail, there is little you can do to guarantee quality other than buy from a reputable company. This may be the only way to be sure that you get the varieties you particularly fancy. On the other hand, when you buy from a nursery or garden centre where you can select the plants yourself, you can choose not only variety but also quality. There are certain things you should keep in mind.

The rose plant that you buy will be either budded or on its own roots. A budded plant has a bud from one variety grafted or budded onto a rootstock of another. Strong, vigorous rootstocks are usually chosen to give a robust plant, especially when the budded variety is a weak grower. This often means a larger but more expensive plant than one on its own roots. Nearly all hybrid teas and floribundas sold are grown this way.

All standard or tree roses must be grown as budded plants. Sometimes two buds are used to give a more evenly spaced head. The varieties are exactly the same as those grown as bush roses, but instead of being budded at ground level they are budded higher up the stem. They may be only 40 or 50 cm tall or large weeping standards on

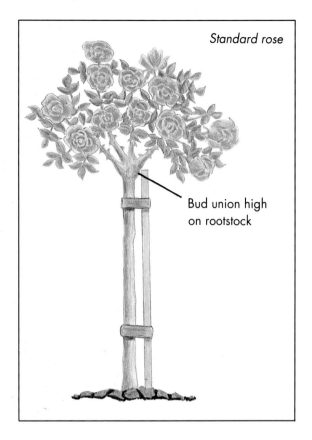

Standard rose

Bud union high
on rootstock

will encourage the plant to branch. Beware of barely rooted cuttings. If in doubt about single stems without growth, turn the container over and check that root growth is obvious.

The way in which you plant your roses and the time of the year when this is done will depend upon whether you purchase budded or own-root plants. Budded roses have traditionally been sold as bare-root plants in the winter when the rose is dormant. Some bare-root roses will be bought in a pot or bag but are placed there only to prevent the roots from drying out before the rose is planted. You can easily check if this is so. When ready to plant, grasp the rose by the stem and lift it bag and all. If the bag falls away, treat the plant as bare root and shake off the remains of the mix it was in. If it stays in the bag, it has probably been growing there for some time and should be treated as a container-grown rose.

1.8-m stems. All standard roses must be staked.

Own-root plants are grown from cuttings. While they may be smaller at the time of purchase, within a year or two they will be as large as a budded plant. They often make more bushy plants and have the advantage that all growth, even from below ground level, is true to variety. Whatever grows is rose! Most own-root roses are sold growing in a container. Nearly all of the types of roses discussed in this book make satisfactory own-root plants.

Ideally, container-grown plants will have been cut back some time before sale to encourage growth. Look for branched plants with growth from low on the bush. Try to avoid a plant which is just a bloom on a stem. Use the flower as an indication of the colour, but choose a bushy plant if possible. If single stem plants are the only ones available remember that tipping back

Planting container-grown roses

Container-grown roses can, in theory, be planted at any time. They seem to do best when planted in the spring after the soil has begun to warm up and the roots are actively growing. Early autumn is also a good time, as this allows the roots to become established and make some growth before the winter. There won't be much top growth, but in the spring the plant will come away very quickly. Don't plant in the cold of the winter. Miniature roses with small roots can suffer from root rot if planted into cold, wet ground.

The plant should be thoroughly watered the day before it is to be planted. Prepare the ground in the normal way and when ready to plant, dig a hole large enough for the rose in its container. The surrounding area should have been well cultivated to a sufficient depth for the roots to grow easily. The root system may seem small when

'Sequoia Gold' is a bushy miniature rose, so when planting give it plenty of space.

planting, but given the right conditions it will soon grow much larger. Check that the container fits into the hole with the top of the soil at the same level or just below the surface of your garden soil. Remove the plant carefully from the container, interfering with the roots as little as possible. Then, keeping as much soil around the roots as you can, place the plant in the hole and fill in firmly around the edges.

Planting bare-root budded roses

The rose that you get from the nursery or garden centre will probably need some attention before you plant it. Check the top of the plant and cut back any broken stems to a good bud. Many growers do this to all stems, especially where a long stub has been left above the top bud, or the top bud is pointing in the wrong direction. Others plant the bush, and cut back later once growth has started.

The roots may also need some attention. Damaged roots should be trimmed back and long, straggling roots shortened a little. The top of the plant should be cut to balance the roots. Large, strong top growth needs large, strong roots. Strong, plentiful top growth on a weak root system needs to be thinned out.

When planting your roses, dig a hole wider and deeper than it appears you will need. Your rose should be planted with the bud union at about soil level. In windy or very cold areas the bud union is sometimes left just below the surface to give extra stability and protection, but it is better if it is just above, as the light encourages more basal breaks. Form a mound of soil in the bottom of the hole to support the plant and spread the roots around it.

Begin filling the hole with good soil, which may include a mixture of peat

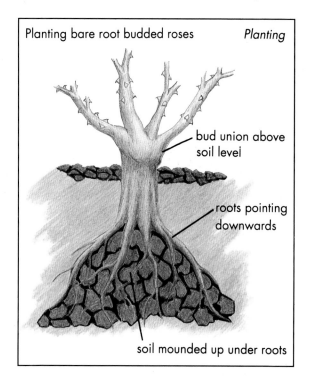

Planting bare root budded roses   *Planting*

bud union above soil level

roots pointing downwards

soil mounded up under roots

and/or old compost. Firm it around the roots as you go. Be careful not to damage the plant or the roots with the heel of your boot if you favour treading a plant in. Before the hole has been completely filled you may need to water the plant in. If the ground is at all dry, pour water into the hollow which remains to settle the soil around the roots and prevent them drying out. If planting in the winter and the weather is likely to be very cold, mound some soil around the canes to give any extra pro-

tection needed.

Standard roses should be planted in the same way as other budded roses, but before covering the roots put in a strong stake. Be careful not to damage the roots. When planting is completed, tie the stem carefully to the stake. The top tie is the most important; if this breaks the stem may bend and break at a lower tie. For this reason, some growers use only a single top tie on short standards.

If the weather has been wet and cold you may wish to postpone planting your new roses. Don't plant into very wet or frozen soil. Roses can be kept for some time in the container in which they are purchased as long as they are not allowed to dry out, or they may be heeled into the ground if they are bare root. To heel in, dig a trench in some unused spot in the garden, place the rose roots in the hole and cover them with soil. Make sure they are well covered and kept moist until you need them.

Pay careful attention to your newly planted roses over the few weeks following planting. Don't let the ground around your plants become too dry if there is no rain. With a few warm days, and especially any warm winds, your new roses can quickly become dehydrated if the soil around their roots dries out.

Chapter 11

PESTS AND DISEASES

'Make Believe'

IT is sad but true that the better you grow your roses the more insect pests you are likely to have. They seem to favour the new green growth and buds on well-grown plants.

How to control these pests is a decision all rose growers have to make for themselves. Many are happy to spray and a variety of commercial products is available for use by the home gardener. Most of these are relatively safe if used carefully according to the directions given, but they are poisons and should be treated as such.

An increasing number of growers prefer not to use these materials and are turning to organic controls. Natural insect sprays are becoming available. Their effect is not as long lasting as the 'chemical' sprays but they are completely safe to use and there is no risk of damage to the environment.

Some are based upon natural fatty acids and I am reminded of my mother throwing soapy water from the weekly wash over the roses to get rid of the greenfly. (I did hear that it doesn't kill them but it gets in their eyes, and when they let go of the stems to rub their eyes they fall and break their necks!)

How frequently you spray and what you spray with will in part depend upon how much disease and damage to your roses you are prepared to tolerate. Rose exhibitors spray frequently as they require clean, disease-free foliage. You may decide not to spray at all. While insect numbers are small, finger and thumb is a useful method of control. Predatory insects like the ladybird, praying mantis or the hover fly larvae will feed upon the pests. Encourage birds into the garden and they too will help to control insects. Natural controls can keep problems in check, but they do not completely remove them.

If you have no objection to other plants among your roses, try some companion planting. Marigolds help to control eel worms and nematodes and garlic is reputed to control greenfly. Mixed planting encourages beneficial insects into the garden. While you may not consider spiders and beetles beneficial insects, researchers at Lincoln University near Christchurch, New Zealand, suggest the formation of 'beetle banks' and 'spider strips' to provide habitats that encourage predatory insects and spider populations. In particular, these insects need a warm, dry place where they can hibernate over winter.

Much more attractive and pleasant is the use of flowering plants. Local studies have shown that phacelia (also known as tansy leaf) attracts our native hover fly which needs flowers for pollen and nectar. In return the larvae of the hover fly prey on the greenfly. We have seen that a mixed garden of roses and other plants, including phacelia, lavender, catmint and other flowering plants, had far fewer greenfly than did a garden with just roses.

New natural controls are being developed all the time. There are predator mites to devour the mites which damage the foliage of roses in greenhouses, but not all the pests may be eaten; a balance must be reached or the predator will starve. A bacterium has been found which affects only caterpillars and when eaten by them acts upon the creature's stomach and kills it. Experiments have been made with pheromones to attract male beetles which can then be trapped and destroyed. Perhaps one day we will live with our roses in a spray-free world.

If you do decide to spray make sure you use the right type of material. If you have an insect problem it is no use spraying with a fungicide, which only controls fungal diseases. If you have rust, a fungicide which only controls mildew will not help. Fortunately most insecticides control many of the common insects and there are general purpose fungicides that will control the few basic disease problems. Combination sprays are available where insecticide and fungicide are already mixed so that from one container on your shelf you can control most of the problems that may arise in your rose garden.

Little mention is made in this book of specific spray material. These are changing all the time and availability varies from country to country. Any reliable garden centre should be able to recommend a suitable product. If you have real problems with your roses try to contact the rose society in your area for advice.

Use your spray equipment carefully and efficiently. Make sure you cover the foliage on the plant, but don't waste spray by having too much run-off onto the ground. Direct the spray upwards to ensure you reach the underside of the leaves. Read the labels on the containers carefully and follow their instructions. Using sprays is one case where 'if a little is good a lot will be better' is not true. Keep spray material out of the reach of children and never put it into unmarked containers. Don't buy more spray than you can use in a season or two. Some sprays have a limited shelf life. Dispose of empty and old spray containers carefully.

Insects

A universal problem in the rose garden is the *greenfly* or *rose aphid*. These familiar insects are particularly common on the growing tips and buds during spring and at other times when the roses are growing well. They sometimes vary in colour to match the reddish tones of the new growth where they are feeding. Several good insec-

Greenfly are a problem in rose gardens around the world, but they can be controlled.

ticides are available for their control.

A number of different *caterpillars* may feed on roses, eating the leaves and sometimes tunnelling into the unopened bud. They arrive early in the spring as the new leaves begin to appear and may join two leaves together or wrap a leaf around themselves for protection as they eat. When this happens, a simple contact spray will not reach them. Use a systemic insecticide which is absorbed into the sap system and kills as they chew, or resort to the use of finger and thumb whenever you see one.

Some *beetles* will attack roses. New Zealand has its grass grub beetle, England the rose beetle and chafer, and parts of North America the Japanese beetle. While a heavy infestation of the larvae in the ground may injure the root system, the more obvious damage is done to the

blooms and the leaves by the feeding of the flying adult. The grass grub beetle flies in the late spring and, where it is common, as night falls the air can be alive with its movement and the sound of its wings. It is difficult to spray in the dark and one year it made a real mess of our roses. We were advised to use a synthetic pyrethroid which has a deterrent action as well as killing on contact. The information on the container promises that some insects will starve to death rather than eat leaves sprayed with the contents. Perhaps it is true. It only takes one spraying in the spring when the first beetle appears and there is no further problem. Perhaps there is a similar material available to you.

In hot, dry conditions or in a greenhouse, *mites* can be a problem. Sometimes wrongly known as red spider, they live on the underside of leaves and a colony will spin a fine silken web. They are minute and hard to see with the naked eye. The damage

Hot, dry conditions are favoured by spider mites, seen here on the underside of this leaf. Watering from below will often help control them.

they do as they feed on the chlorophyll will show on the upper surface as a yellow marbling of the leaf. They don't like water and watering from below will help to control them. Some insecticides give partial control and special miticides are available for severe infestations.

There are other insect pests which may be found only on one part of the plant. *Thrips*, a very small black fly, may damage the petals. After pruning, all cuts thicker than a pencil may need to be sealed to prevent *stem borer* entering the cane. The froth of *cuckoo-spit* or *frog hopper* may appear in the garden. This insect seems to prefer small roses, as the closer leaves give more places for it to nestle. Unless you use a systemic insecticide, the froth must be washed off with the hose before spraying. This will expose a yellowish creature — the young frog hopper — which can then be picked off by hand or sprayed.

Of course there are larger pests, sometimes as large as browsing deer! Fences and screens can be a protection if the problem becomes severe, and we have heard of low two-wire electric fences being used around precious rose gardens by some country growers. Recently we had a problem with hares eating newly planted willow trees. This was solved by spraying a mix of natural resin and egg powder over and around the trees. Some of the spray reached a few roses and it did them no harm. It is not poisonous and it certainly kept the hares away.

Diseases

Like many other plants, roses are susceptible to some fungal diseases, and this problem requires a different approach. Here prevention is better than cure; it is better to spray before there are any symptoms, for once a plant is infected the fungus is very difficult to cure. In extreme cases the only remedy may be to prune off the severe damage and spray to protect the new growth. Nothing can repair the foliage damage caused by most fungal diseases.

While local conditions will affect the severity and range, there are a few common diseases which are likely to be encountered in most places.

Black spot can defoliate a plant. A roughly circular spot rather like a drop of dye on absorbent material appears on the upper surface of the leaf. As it gets larger the surrounding area turns yellow and the leaf drops off. Black spot is especially associated with warmth and humidity. Fortunately, as with all the common diseases, there are a number of sprays which will prevent the disease if used before it appears.

A curling of the leaves and a white fungus on new leaves and buds signals the arrival of *powdery mildew*. It particularly occurs in draughty places and at times when warm days change rapidly to cool nights. Spraying can prevent any further spread but cannot cure the damaged foliage.

In recent years both home gardeners and a research unit at Massey University, New Zealand, have been experimenting with the use of baking soda (sodium bicarbonate) for the control of powdery mildew. Reports are all positive, and some results have been better than those using a standard fungicide. Try baking soda at the rate of 2 g (just less than a level teaspoonful) per litre of water. You must use a wetting agent or light spraying oil with it, again at the rate of one teaspoonful per litre of water, as baking soda alone is not effective. You will also need to spray more often — about every 10 days.

Rust is a disease of hot, dry weather. If small yellow spots appear on the surface of a leaf look on the underside. If you find an orange powder you have rust. It will gradually spread and may turn black, while the leaf will turn yellow and drop off. It can be controlled with a suitable spray, but before the infestation spreads too far the affected leaves should be picked off and destroyed.

Botrytis blight is a problem of cool, moist conditions. During periods of continuous damp weather buds may fail to open and become covered with a greyish mould, which, if not removed, can affect neighbouring leaves and stems. It is easily controlled and a change in weather or increasing the ventilation in a greenhouse may be all that is necessary.

I had always thought that *downy mildew* was a new arrival, but a recently acquired copy of the Royal National Rose Society booklet, *The Enemies of the Rose*, 1910 edition, describes Rose Black Mildew (*Peronospora sparsa*) which is the same disease. 'Young vigorous leaves suddenly commence to wilt and fall in showers if the branch is slightly shaken, the young shoots also droop and die back.' Fortunately it is still not common. It may occur in a warm, humid greenhouse or where similar conditions are found outside. Grey purplish stains will show on affected leaves and it can attack green stems. It is the suddenness of the attack and the rapidity of spread which is frightening.

It is easily controlled with modern sprays and if you follow a regular spray programme there should be no problem with any of these fungal diseases. When spraying, it is a good idea to alternate fungicides as some diseases can build up a resistance.

There is little you can do about fungal diseases if you don't wish to spray. Some varieties of roses are more resistant to disease than others. You could grow only these, but this will limit your selection and even then you will still have some prob-

lems from time to time. Garden hygiene will help. Do not allow dead and diseased leaves to collect among the branches of your roses; and remove fallen leaves from the ground. Keep the rose beds free from weeds and use a mulch to prevent dirty water from splashing up onto the lower leaves when it rains.

Mottled and distorted leaves can be caused by viruses, which are usually spread by contact. They cannot be controlled by spraying. There is some disagreement about

If rust is a problem and the leaves are turning yellow, they should be picked off and destroyed before it spreads.

how much damage the common viruses do to roses, but badly infected plants should be removed from the garden and destroyed. No propagation should be done from any infected plant.

Don't confuse viral infection with the discolouration of leaves caused by a deficiency of some element in the soil and therefore related to fertilizer and feeding.

Chapter 12

PRUNING

'Figurine'

'I was always a hard pruner and took a pride in the fact. When I had finished with a bed ... it was not obvious at first glance that anything at all was growing in it ...
The Roses were excellent. But the point is that now the bushes are not being pruned at all and the Roses are still excellent. It is all very strange.'

Fletcher's Folly – H.L.V. Fletcher

WE have often wondered how large a miniature rose bush would grow if it was never pruned. We have seen plants that we expect to be perhaps a metre high growing 2 m up a trellis and, in Sydney, miniature roses growing under cover for cut-flower production are at least twice as high as we would expect. Of course the conditions under which the plant is grown will affect its size, but so too will the amount of prun-ing or lack of pruning that the rose receives.

What you want from a rose will also influence how it is pruned. In general, light pruning gives more flowers on shorter growth, while hard pruning gives longer stems but fewer flowers. The gardener who wants colour in the garden may give a light trim. The exhibitor and the cut flower grower prune hard. But hard pruning will not give long stems on roses that do not naturally grow that way and tall roses cannot be made short. Every rose has a natural minimum height to which it wants to grow under the prevailing conditions. Cutting it hard only removes potential flowers and results in new growth as the plant tries to grow again.

Roses are usually pruned while they are dormant because at this time the sap is not

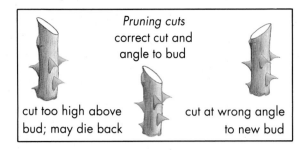

Pruning cuts
correct cut and
angle to bud

cut too high above
bud; may die back

cut at wrong angle
to new bud

flowing and the cut stems do not bleed. This means winter pruning is the rule.

Too often new rose plants are pruned too hard in the first few years. If too much of the stronger growth is removed in the early years the rose may never have a chance to show its potential.

In general, pruning is done to shape the plant and at the same time encourage new growth which in turn results in more flowers. Although pruning is an art, it is not difficult, as there are so many variations that it is hard to go wrong. While different types of roses should be pruned in different ways, there are certain basic rules that apply to all.

Begin by removing any dead or dying stems. Cut them back hard to healthy growth. From time to time, as necessary, thin out some of the oldest growth from the base of the bush to make room for new growth and to prevent the plant from becoming too woody. Always cut back to healthy wood. Check the colour of the pith in the cut stem. In colder areas frost may have damaged last year's growth, which may look healthy on the outside but have damaged brown pith in the centre. If this is the case, cut further down the stem until undamaged growth is found.

If dead blooms and flower heads are removed as they occur, many small roses will need little winter pruning other than that already mentioned. This applies to upright growing miniature and patio roses. Make sure that any stronger shoots which have borne large flower heads have been

cut back by about a third, and that as necessary twiggy growth has been thinned out and tipped back.

Climbing roses put out long, strong shoots which form the framework of the bush. These should not be cut while they are growing unless the size is getting out of hand. Upright climbers should have lateral growth thinned and cut back to stop the plant becoming overcrowded.

Ground-cover roses should be thought of as prostrate climbers. The long growth is the framework of the plant. Tip lateral growth but cut other healthy growth only when the plant becomes too large.

Once-flowering roses should be pruned as soon after flowering as possible. Apart from tipping back lateral flowering stems and basic pruning very little need be done. From time to time cut back the main growth by about a third.

Mention must be made of the pruning trials conducted by the Royal National Rose Society in their gardens at St Albans, England. Bushes of one variety in the same bed have been pruned by three different methods. One-third have been pruned in the traditional English way by hard pruning; one-third have been pruned lightly and the remainder pruned with hedge clippers. Several different varieties have been treated in this way. To date, observation has shown that the best results in terms of quantity of flowers have been obtained from those pruned with the hedge clippers. A further experiment has shown that this may be because the non-flowering twiggy growth which is not removed by the hedge clippers gives more leaves on the plant, which in turn produce more nourishment for growth. The gardener at St Albans expects that from time to time the old and dead growth on the roses pruned with the hedge clippers will have to be removed in the usual way, but even if this is every three or four years, pruning time and effort will

RUGUL

Pruning not only shapes the plant, it encourages new growth and flowers. Both 'Rugul' and 'Gentle Touch', seen here in the Queen Mary Rose Garden, Regents Park, London, have benefited from such pruning.

have been reduced considerably.

These experiments have great implications for the way we prune our roses. If you want long-stemmed roses for a vase or for exhibiting continue to prune in the normal way as described above. If colour in the garden is your main interest you may like to carry out some trials of your own. If you do, make sure that falling leaves and petals are not allowed to collect among the stems of your miniature roses. Rotting material hides insect pests and harbours disease. Remember to practise good garden hygiene.

Whatever you decide about pruning and how it should be done, don't be afraid to do it yourself. Successful pruning is largely observation. Decide what you want from your roses and prune to achieve this. Watch the way your roses grow. If you achieve your aim, continue to prune in the same way. Remember the difference between good and bad pruning is a summer's growth.

Chapter 13

THE ROSE YEAR

'Old Glory'

Spring

SPRING is a great time in the rose garden whatever type of roses you grow. Established roses have been pruned and the beds tidied. New varieties may have been planted and there is a feeling of expectation in the air as new growth begins and you look forward to another season of flowers.

Give your roses a feed. In wet, cold areas wait until the ground warms up before you do this. Dormant plants cannot make use of the fertilizer, and rain can leach much of it from the soil before it can be used. Any good general fertilizer is satisfactory, but check that it has the full range of NPK (nitrogen, phosphorus and potassium).

The best time to apply a mulch if you intend using one is as the ground gets warmer. Get it on before there is too much soft new growth which might be damaged as you work among the roses. Keep it back from the stems of small roses as fungus from the decomposing mulch may affect the plant. Many materials, ranging from farmyard manure to stack bottom to bark, can be used as a mulch, but check your source of supply before it is spread. Has the grass or straw been sprayed with a weed killer or is the sawdust from treated timber? If the answer is yes, it does not belong on your rose beds.

In nearly every case a mulch is not a replacement for fertilizer. It will certainly improve the texture of the soil and encourage worms as it decays, but many mulches add little in the way of nutrients to the soil. On the contrary, some materials like sawdust or straw use nitrogen in the decaying process and actually remove nitrogen from

'The Fairy'

the soil as they begin to break down. Nitrogen is returned to the soil later, but it is a good idea to use a little blood and bone or other nitrogenous fertilizer with dry organic mulches.

Don't be lulled into a false sense of security. In colder areas it is the late spring frost that causes the most damage to roses. If this happens, cut back to healthy growth and start again. Some damage may not be obvious but will show up later as unexpected weak growth. If this occurs, trim back at this time. When badly damaged, own-root roses can be cut back almost to ground level and they will grow again, but budded plants need at least one or two buds left above the crown. If you grow small roses in a very cold place and need to give them some cover, don't be fooled by a false spring and uncover them too soon.

Spring is a good time to plant new con-

tainer-grown miniature and patio roses. As soon as the ground warms up sufficiently to encourage root growth they can be put in. If the new plants have been growing under cover and have soft new growth they should be gradually hardened off before planting them in an open garden. Newly planted roses must not be allowed to get too dry.

Growth is very fast at this time of the year. It is the new soft growth on the roses that greenfly love and small caterpillars may be feeding in the growing tips of the expanding buds. Begin to spray for these pests as soon as they appear. If you use a combination all-purpose spray you will prevent fungal diseases as well.

Water as required. It has been said that rapidly growing roses need about 2 cm of water a week. This is a lot of water and if it does not occur naturally you need to irrigate.

If you have been carefully following all

'Fairhope'

the advice and watering deeply and your roses are still not growing well, perhaps the pH of your soil is wrong. The pH is the measure of soil acidity. Roses do best in a neutral soil with a pH of about 6.5 to 7.0. Now would be a good time to have the pH checked. If it needs correcting for roses ask for advice on how best this can be done.

Many districts have spring rose shows. Try to visit one in your area. This is an excellent opportunity to see new and unfamiliar varieties, but do remember that the best roses in the show may not be the best for your garden. Ask for advice if you have any doubts.

Summer

The first flush of bloom should be over. Roses left to wither on the bush should be removed and the garden will look much neater if this is done before the petals fall.

Cutting the stem with the spent bloom back to a true leaf (it often has five leaflets but sometimes more) will encourage new growth and with it more flowers.

Don't cut blooms with long stems from new bushes. Remember that a rose feeds through its leaves, so keep as many healthy leaves as possible on new or weak bushes. The plants need a chance to grow and build up a strong framework for the future. Some growers even suggest preventing new bushes from flowering in the spring in order to conserve energy within the bush for future growth. We can never do this. I want to see the new blooms. But we do take only very short stems when removing dead flowers.

Once-blooming roses should be pruned as they finish flowering. They usually

'Ring of Fire'

flower on second-year wood and pruning now encourages new growth which will carry flowers next spring. Winter pruning is likely to remove some of this growth and reduce the number of flowers.

If you want your roses to continue to grow over the summer, they should be fed after the first flush of flowers. Remember that small bushes require smaller quantities of fertilizer, and too much may encourage lush growth without increasing the number of flowers. For miniature roses, a teaspoonful of fertilizer worked into the soil on two or three occasions over the summer is better than too much at one time.

In many areas the most important thing to do over the next few months is to ensure that your roses have adequate water. A good soaking is better than several light sprinklings as it encourages the roots to go deeper. Use your favourite effective method but remember that water will mark some blooms. On the other hand, I am sure roses benefit from an overhead water occasionally. It helps to keep the leaves clean and controls some pests.

If you have severe water restrictions in midsummer you may need to let your roses go into a form of summer dormancy. Give them enough water to keep them alive but do not remove spent blooms or cut them back in any way. You do not want to encourage new growth. You may be able to recycle some water for use on your garden. When you want your roses to come back into growth give them a thorough soaking and a day or two later cut them back and feed. New growth will soon begin and within a few weeks you will have fresh blooms.

Summer is the time to enjoy your roses: 'Rosie' (above) and 'Pink Bells' (opposite).

In this way it is also possible to time blooms for a special occasion. You do need local knowledge about how long it takes from cutting back to blooming, but with this knowledge it is easy to work back from the desired date to find the day on which the summer trimming should be done. Different types of roses will respond at different times and of course the weather can also affect blooming times. Spread your summer trimming over several days to allow for this.

The hot days of summer encourage fungal diseases among our roses. This is especially true if you also suffer with high humidity. Keep your preventative spray programme going. In hot, dry areas mites may be a problem. If your usual insecticide does not control them, you should consider a specific miticide. Remember mites do not like water and watering the leaves from

below can help.

Climbers will be putting out long new growth which adds to the framework of the plant. While the canes are still soft they can be easily trained into the places where they are needed. Tie them in carefully as the growing tips can easily snap off.

On budded plants, watch for growth from below the bud union. Known as suckers, these come from the understock and drain nourishment from the true growth. They will have a different leaf not just a different colour and they need to be carefully removed, not just cut off. Remember own-root roses have no suckers and new growth from ground level and below is the true variety.

Autumn

Cooler temperatures and shorter sunshine hours give deeper colours to the blooms. They also have time to grow larger.

As the days become cooler and winter approaches there is no need to remove those last spent blooms. We don't want soft, new grow on the bushes when the first frosts hit. There is little value in cutting back to encourage growth which will have no opportunity to produce blooms before winter arrives. On the other hand, in damp conditions don't let flowers rot on the bush as they will produce botrytis spores which can infect and kill the stems. At this time just snap them off.

For similar reasons, do not apply nitrogenous fertilizer. Let your roses begin to harden off so they are better prepared for the winter. Some extra potash can help this hardening process.

Insects and some diseases can still be a problem. Continue to spray as necessary while there is still time for blooms to open. Make sure your roses are in good condition as they go into the winter and you will get better results in the spring.

Now is a good time to assess your roses. Do you really get equal value from all of them? Is there one that is always the first to get mildew? No matter what you do another always defoliates with black spot? And then there is that one that only has a few flowers and they always ball in the rain. These are the roses you might decide to discard.

Don't be too eager to throw away new bushes. They deserve two or three years to show what they can do. And there are always some roses which are grown for sentimental reasons.

If you intend removing a bush from an existing rose bed, it is not too soon to do it now. Remove the bush and at least some of the soil in which it has been growing. This is particularly important if the bush has been infected with a virus. Leave the hole and let the sun and weather get to it for a while.

New roses usually do not do well if planted straight into soil where roses have been growing for some time. It is uncertain whether this is due to a toxin or just soil depletion. Sun and air help. So does compost worked into the ground where the new bush is to go several weeks before planting. Fill the hole with fresh soil or compost and do this before the ground gets too cold and damp.

The preparation of new rose beds should also begin in the autumn, especially if they are to be dug out of lawn or unused ground. Make sure they are as free as possible from perennial weeds (spray with a weed killer if necessary) and rough dig to at least two spade depths. Compost can be dug in at this time or left until the weather has worked on the ground for a few weeks. Cultivating it into the soil after a few weeks also helps to control the first crop of weeds. Let the new bed settle and it will be ready for the new roses when they arrive.

New bare-root roses should be ordered. If there are particular varieties that you must have they need to be ordered in advance. Order directly from the grower or from your favourite garden centre, but don't just leave it to chance. Many popular and new varieties sell out quickly.

A rose which is not doing well in your garden may have been planted in the wrong place. It may need more sun, more shelter or just a change of soil in another part of the garden. Giving it a walk in the wheelbarrow can sometimes help. Autumn is a good time to move roses. It gives them a chance to settle into their new site before the cold of winter. Care for them and plant like new bareroot roses. Remember the top must be trimmed to match the loss of root.

'Little Nugget' in the Manurewa Trial Grounds, New Zealand.

Winter

I well remember a Norwegian rose grower who each year experiences a bitter winter saying, 'Winter! That's a terrible time,' but for those of us who do not suffer in this way this is the time to plant new bareroot roses and to prune existing bushes.

If you have roses on order they should be arriving any day. If they are from a reputable nurseryman they will be well packed and should not have dried out in transit. Even so it is as well to check them over on arrival. If you will be planting them within a day or two, and the roots are moist and the canes show no sign of shrinking, they may be safely repacked or kept in a cool place under a damp sack or newspaper.

If the plants have dried out, soak the roots overnight in a bucket of water. If they are badly dried out and the canes show severe shrinkage you may save them by burying the whole plant in damp soil. Leave for two or three weeks, watching all the time that the soil remains moist. Canes and roots which have become dehydrated and shrunk have an opportunity to absorb moisture from the ground. The plant will come to no harm and may even begin to grow new roots.

Whatever you do with your new roses, don't leave the roots exposed to the air for any longer than is absolutely neccessary, for the fine feeding hair roots of the plant dry out very quickly.

Read again the section on planting roses.

In most places there is no best time for pruning. Particularly in colder areas, it is the frost and weather which determine when your roses come into bloom, not when they are pruned.

Don't begin too early. Wait at least until

the bushes begin to lose their leaves after the first hard frosts. You don't want to encourage new growth which can be damaged by later cold weather. Once the bush has become dormant it is safe to prune. If you live in an area where late frosts are common, wait until the bushes show signs of growth but don't leave it until the new shoots are several centimetres long. This wastes the energy of the bush as it produces new growth which is going to be cut off.

In mild places with no frost, where the roses are never truly dormant and never lose their leaves, choose the time when they are making the least growth. This will probably be in the winter, and by timing your pruning you can have some control over the flowering of your roses.

To be sure of healthy summer roses you must do some winter spraying. The old familiar products are still the most popular. Lime sulphur gives a good clean up and helps to take off the last of the leaves. Don't use it at other times when the plants are in growth and covered with leaves! I find that spraying with winter oil and copper after the roses have been pruned helps to seal over the pruning cuts. Clean up the ground around your roses before spraying and spray the ground close to your bushes as well as the bush itself to kill off any disease spores that may be on decaying leaves near the surface.

In areas of extreme cold where roses need winter protection, gather your covering material before the worst of the winter arrives. Some trimming of the bush to cut out dead wood and shorten long growth may be done if this will make it easier to protect the bush and bring it through the winter. As the cold weather approaches, cover your bushes as necessary. Remember it is the wind chill which is the greatest killer and protection from winds is most important. Roses in containers can be taken into a garage or basement that does not freeze.

Do not be in too much hurry to uncover your roses completely as the days begin to warm up. Harden them off by exposing them a little at a time and be prepared to cover again if a cold snap occurs. Complete your pruning when the covers have finally gone, checking carefully for frost damage and cutting back to healthy wood. An advantage of own-root roses is that they can be frosted to the ground and still have strong new growth reappear from the roots.

Planting of new roses must also wait until the ground thaws and begins to warm up. As long as they are kept moist (not wet), rose plants can be kept for some time in a cold but frost-free shed.

Chapter 14

OUR CHOICE

A good proven variety – 'Rainbow's End'.

IN our first book we included a short list of favourites, and to avoid arguments we did His and Hers lists. This created a lot of comment and so we have decided to finish with the same again. No discussion; no comparison; just two lists. A rose that appears twice must be good!

Good Proven Varieties

His	*Hers*
Jean Kenneally	Dorola
Jeanne Lajoie	Jean Kenneally
Magic Carrousel	Jeanne Lajoie
Minnie Pearl	Little Jackie
Moonlight Lady	Minnie Pearl
Patio Prince	Moonlight Lady
Pink Petticoat	Patio Flame
Rainbow's End	Ragtime
Rise 'n' Shine	Sachet
Sachet	Why Not

Promising Varieties

His	*Hers*
Aoraki	Aoraki
Irresistible	Cream Puff
Lucky Me	Irresistible
Mother's Love	Kapiti
Patio Queen	Little Nugget
Pierrine	Lucky Me
Pretty Polly	Mother's Love
Rexy's Baby	Panache
Silver	Patio Queen
Snow Twinkle	Pierrine

GLOSSARY

bare root roses Usually budded roses with no soil around their roots which are dug from the ground in the winter.

basal shoot A strong shoot from low on the plant.

bud union The place where the bud has been joined to the rootstock.

calyx The cup-shaped base of the flower which later holds the seeds.

climbing rose A rose producing very long growth from its base. This growth needs support and frequently does not flower in its first year.

dead-heading Removing faded and dead flowers to encourage new growth.

floribunda Typically, a rose with many blooms to a stem.

form The shape of the bloom.

fungicide A substance to control fungal diseases.

heel in Put plants temporarily into the ground.

hip/hep The fruit or seed pod of the rose.

hybrid tea Rose with large blooms, usually with many petals and often classic rose form. It usually has only a few blooms per flowering stem.

insecticide A substance to control insect pests.

miticide A substance to control mites.

mulch A layer of material laid over the soil to conserve moisture, reduce summer temperatures and suppress weeds.

own-root roses Roses grown from cuttings on their own roots.

pistil Female reproductive part of the flower.

polyantha Rose with abundant small flowers in clusters.

rootstock Plant onto which the wanted variety is budded.

species The ancient wild roses from which all newer roses have originated.

sport A vegetative mutation of a plant which creates a noticeable difference in form, growth or colour. Some climbers are sports of bush roses.

stamen Male reproductive organ of a flower.

sucker A growth from below the bud union.

systemic spray A spray which is absorbed into the plant's system.

true leaf In roses, a leaf that has five or more leaflets.

understock *see* rootstock

variety A variety of rose raised in cultivation; not a species rose. A cultivar.

INDEX